M000188300

How I Met My Mother

How I Met My Mother . . .

**. . . and the four
brothers I never
knew I had**

Charles Cornacchio

How I Met My Mother:
And the Four Brothers I Never Knew I Had

Copyright © 2014 Charles Cornacchio. All rights reserved.
No part of this book may be reproduced or retransmitted in
any form or by any means without the written permission
of the publisher.

Published by Wheatmark®
1760 East River Road, Suite 145,
Tucson, Arizona 85718 USA
www.wheatmark.com

ISBN: 978-1-62787-058-0 (paperback)
ISBN: 978-1-62787-059-7 (ebook)

LCCN: 2013954246

This is a true account of the events leading up to meeting my birth mother and discovering the four brothers I never knew I had. While the principle names are true, some of the supporting names have been changed to protect their identity.

Prologue

I PULLED INTO THE PARKING lot of the apartment complex where my birth mother lived, not knowing for sure what was about to happen. Would this be as simple as a one-time meet-and-greet? A "courtesy call ending" to my natural curiosity about who I was and where I came from, with answers to the questions I've had about my past? Either way, I knew my life was about to change forever.

As my newfound brother and I rode the elevator up to her fourth floor in uncomfortable silence, I began to think about how this would not only change my life, but also the lives of others. I wondered what it might mean for Emily, my adoptive mother and the only woman I knew as my "real mother," and for my beautiful wife, MaryAnn, and our four children.

We stepped out of the elevator into a hallway that seemed as long as a football field—eerily long—like a camera shot in a psychological thriller. The door to my birth mother's apartment was straight ahead. Although we walked with purpose, it seemed to take forever to get there. I watched as my new brother reached down and slowly turned the knob, all the while looking at me as if knowing how monumental a moment this was. Then the door to my birth mother's apartment opened ...

I Was Eight

IT WAS JULY OF 1962. I remember the moment so vividly. I was standing in the kitchen of our Bronx row house when my mother approached me with a piece of paper in her hand. She seemed troubled. "There's something you should know," she said. Could the paper be a note from school? A report from the doctor? Did I draw something inappropriate? My mother continued with the directness of a woman on a mission, as if this was something she had to do, and she wanted it to be over. "You were adopted," she said in a matter-of-fact tone.

This revelation should have been shocking, but as an eight-year-old who was very comfortable in his surroundings, I was innocently curious. I had the typical questions focusing on who my parents were, where they are now, and why I was given up for adoption. But my mother was quick to keep the information coming, answering my questions directly so we didn't have to talk much more about it. I felt her uneasiness and discomfort in having this conversation. She had waited for the right moment to unveil the truth that she'd held onto for the past eight years. She must have figured that eight years of age was old enough to comprehend but young enough to be indifferent to the news. I also sensed her relief. She had said the words, got it out in the open, and I'm sure it lifted a load off of her mind and heart.

I'm sure she was uncomfortable having this conversation.

My parents were loving and caring people, living a typical middle income life. Both working as bookkeepers for family lumber businesses. Of course, "love" can be displayed in different ways and if you know anything about first generation Bronx Italians then you understand that signs of love don't always present themselves with a universal display of affection, such as a hug or a kiss. They often come in the form of yelling and scolding—a much higher display of care and concern than simply saying "I love you." If you grew up with Italians then you understand. To my parents, it was a safer way than actually having to say those very emotional words.

Wedding photo of Mom and Dad

And they must have really loved me because I got plenty of discipline and punishment in my early years. Still, I knew I was loved and had never before had a thought that I came from anywhere other than this family. So, naturally, when my mother got me caught up on my secret background, I wanted to know all about my real parents. Unfortunately, my mother couldn't provide much detail. I fantasized that they had died in a plane crash. Dramatically, with their final breaths, they reached out to my adoptive parents and said, "Please take care of Charles for us," and then they died.

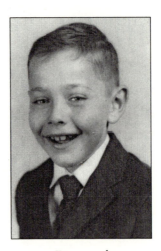

First grade

At least that was the story I would tell my friends at St. Barnabas Elementary School. It sounded good at the time and got the reaction I had hoped for from my female classmates, who found it to be very romantic and endearing. "You poor kid. Losing both your parents and having this nice family take you in as one of their own." Yeah, I was working it at eight. But I always felt that an eight-year-old in the Bronx was the equivalent of a twelve-year-old in any other part of the country.

The truth of the matter, as I was told, was that I was born to a woman who wasn't married. I was a bastard. A love child. Oh, the shame! That's why I liked my story better.

As my mother told it, my biological mother gave birth to me in the "unwed mothers' section" of Misrecordia Hospital in the Bronx.

We lived on East 235th Street, in the Woodlawn section, about a mile from Misrecordia. We passed by that building with the huge cross on the front every time we went to my relatives' houses in Laconia and Wakefield, so I knew it well. After learning this news, passing by that hospital would take on a whole new meaning to me. I examined it each time we passed, wishing I could go back in time to see what was happening in there. It was my only connection to this new past I was quickly learning about.

The paper my mother was holding when she told me about my adoption was my original birth certificate, which bore the name "Paul Henry Cosentino." The fact that my birth name was really Paul was a bigger shock than the fact that these people weren't my real parents. "You mean my name isn't really Charles?" I didn't care for the name at first—especially the middle name, Henry—but I changed my mind about the name Paul eighteen months later when the Beatles debuted on the *Ed Sullivan Show*; I was pretty excited to share the same name with one of the Beatles!

I began to ask new questions, but my mother had no answers for me.

ME: "What was my birth mother like?"

EMILY: "I didn't know her."

ME: "Who do I look like?"

EMILY: "I don't know. We were so excited we

were getting a baby that we didn't really hear a lot of what they said. All I remember was that your mother was young. Her name was Mary, and she was Italian. Your father was English."

Another connection to the Beatles!

ME: "When did you get me?"

EMILY: "You were five months old when we brought you home."

ME: "Where was I before that?"

EMILY: "In an orphanage in the city."

ME: "And that's all you know?"

EMILY: "Yes, that's about it."

ME: "Why did you change my name?"

EMILY: "We wanted to name you Charles after your grandfather."

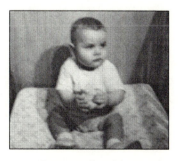

At five months old, 1954

Charles was my grandfather on my adopted father's side. I have a vivid memory of him. He was a small man with white hair and a very thick Italian accent. I was struck by how overwhelmingly affectionate he was towards me. Hugging, kissing, and other outward signs of affection were not that common in our family, but my grandfather was the exception. Kids have a keen sense of when adults truly like them, and Grandpa Cornacchio was a very loving and caring man to me. I think I might have been his favorite!

My grandfather, Charles

He always took an interest in everything I did. When I begged my parents for a guitar, it was my grandfather who stood in my corner, convincing my father to buy one for me. Of course, my father, Matty, was a very practical man and before he made any purchase he made me promise that I would take lessons. I agreed, and he bought me my first guitar. It was an acoustic six-string that came in an odd shaped cardboard box. I remember the smell of the wood and varnish and the sound of the strings when strummed. It just made me feel so complete when I held it. I strummed it every day and night, finding notes and chords through experimentation and chance fingering. I didn't know what I was doing but loved the smell of the guitar and the sound it made.

Following up on my promise to my father, I took two lessons and quit. It was too painful to go through those early lessons of endlessly plucking on one string before moving to another string. I stopped going but didn't tell my parents for weeks. On lesson days I would pack up my guitar in its cardboard box, leave the house, and sit at a soda fountain counter at Tom's Five and Dime store on the corner of Katonah Avenue and 235th, drinking ten-cent chocolate egg creams before returning home with a chocolate mustache. I wasn't a very good sneak, but it still took about three weeks and a phone call from my instructor before my parents found out. I knew I was in trouble and the first thing I said wasn't, "Please don't be mad" or "Please don't punish me." It was, "Please don't tell Grandpa," not because I was afraid he would get angry, but because I was afraid the news would disappoint him. He always asked me to bring my guitar and play when we came to visit. He got a kick out of whatever I was playing, even though we both knew it was not very good. I remember strumming the guitar, playing fake chords while singing fake Italian words to a fake Italian song I just made up on the spot and we would both laugh. I loved that man.

Even though I stopped taking the painful and boring lessons, I still really wanted to learn how to play the guitar. I continued to play by teaching myself and learning chords from some of the older neighborhood kids who had a band. I picked it up very quickly and before long started playing and writing songs. I found it strange that no one else in our family had this passion for a musical instrument, but I liked it and it seemed to give me an identity within the family.

My First Holy Communion with my grandfather, mother Emily, and her mother, Theresa: 1964

I suddenly realized I had a talent I never knew I had and a talent that no other relative in our family had. So here I was, with all this new information about my life and making new realizations about tendencies I hadn't seen earlier. The fact that I didn't look like anyone in the family had never crossed my mind before hearing the news of my adoption, but now seemed blatantly obvious. And there was a traditional dynamic that documented this.

If you understand Italian-American culture in the 1950s and '60s, then you know that every Sunday meant dinner at 2:00 p.m. with about twenty relatives, including grandparents, aunts, uncles, and cousins. The adults would sit at the big table and we were relegated to a folding card table in the living room. Our uncles and fathers would argue about politics, sports, and anything that would provide a heated discussion. The mom's and aunts would try to interject without getting ganged up on by all the men. After dinner it was back to all smiles and someone would always want to take a family picture. Big group shots of a small village of Italians gathered on and around the living room sofa.

Armed with this new information about being adopted, I began to notice that I looked like no one in these pictures. And it came to me that, unlike everyone else in the room, I had no past, no history, and no heritage. I tried my best to fit in and be one of them. The adults were great at making me feel completely accepted, but the cousins on my father's side were a different story. The older boys were pretty cruel about it, as kids at that age can be. They never wanted to include me in things they were doing, and sometimes went out of their way to let me know it.

These times were difficult. It coldly reminded me that I was an outsider. Suddenly, the wonder and curiosity of who my parents were, what they were like, and where they were now became more of my everyday thinking. These questions were always on my mind.

Christmas 1962 with my sister, Helen, and cousins
John, Paul, and Vivian

As I grew older, I found that there were more differences than just appearance. My interests and my behavior were very different from the rest of my family. Most of my family and my extended family were a bunch of worker bees. They carried the kind of prideful work ethic that you so rarely find today.

I, on the other hand, would rather play—a bad word in our family. But not to me. I would rather play stickball, play "off -the-stoop," flip baseball cards, or play with army men than do anything work related. So I was looked down upon and made to feel somewhat guilty about my lack of a work ethic.

"Oh, that Charles," they would lament. "All he wants to do is play," frowning on my immaturity. But the fact is I *was* immature. I was eight!

Still, the pressure to uphold the family work ethic wasn't enough to make me conform. When I was in third grade, I wanted to try out for the youth baseball league. I went to the tryouts by myself and clearly remember standing in the field with all the the other kids who were trying out, and feeling completely alone. All the other kids were getting advice and were being cheered on by a massive collection of parents strung along the sidelines. I watched and wondered what that must feel like. My parents said they were too busy to make it, but I think that was their way of letting me know that they didn't really approve of all this playtime.

I can remember one time that my mother, father, and sister actually came to a game. I remember this game so vividly because it was a rare occurrence.

My mother and sister laughed when I put on my catcher's gear. I could feel their embarrassment but knew it came from never seeing me in catcher's gear before.

At this particular game, I got injured before the first inning even began. I was in my crouched position, ready to warm up the pitcher, when I decided I needed to take off my catcher's mask to adjust the straps. Just then, unaware that I wasn't quite ready, the pitcher released a perfect strike to my head. I fell backward and had to sit out the first three innings.

The only pain I felt was that my family, who finally came to a game, saw me sitting on the bench. I begged the coach to put me in, but he made me wait the standard three innings. I was so afraid my parents were going to leave. When he finally put me in to bat I was so anxious to perform well that even though the first pitch was way over my head I tomahawked at it. And if I hadn't embarrassed them enough already, I was certain that awful swing did the trick. I don't remember them coming to any more games after that. However, I was quite good and made the all-star team. My family did come out to the end-of-season dinner, and I could see how proud they were when my coach said some nice things about me and I received my trophy. It was a memorable night.

Don't get me wrong. It wasn't as though I felt like a complete outcast. Far from it. I just think that sometimes my behavior tested their patience and added to the embarrassment they always seemed to feel.

I was very social and had no problem being the center of attention while everyone else in my family remained humble, introverted, and preferred to be on the sidelines.

Aside from being the only show-off in the family, I was also the only child in our extended family who was chronically ill; I had health problems from the time my parents brought me home from the orphanage.

It was December 23, 1954—an exciting day for my parents—and all the relatives who were anticipating Emily and Matty bringing home their baby boy. What an early Christmas present for Emily and Matthew Cornacchio: a son!

My parents had adopted a girl two years earlier.

Her given name was Helen, and they kept her original name. But the adoption process didn't come without more than a little anxiety. Adopting parents didn't go to the nursery and window shop. They didn't get to pick and choose which baby they'd get. All they could do was designate if they wanted a boy or a girl.

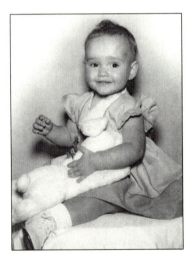

Helen

Emily and Matty were presented with a different baby girl before they received Helen. This first baby had very dark features and tightly curled hair, and while my parents were thrilled to have a child, they thought this baby looked more Hispanic than Italian and were afraid that she wouldn't fit into the family. It was a tenuous situation because Emily and Matty had gone through such an arduous qualification process and didn't want to seem ungrateful. They feared the adoption agency would count the refusal of this baby as a strike against them.

Instead, the agency made arrangements to take the baby back and offered them Helen, a fair-skinned baby with doll-like features that they thought would be a much better match for the family.

⌇

Fast forward two years, and it was time to bring a little boy home. So, on December 23, soon after Emily and Matty received the call to come to the Catholic Charities Orphanage to get their baby boy, all of the relatives came to the house to dote over me as the newest addition to the family. The house was festive and filled with Christmas decorations. The tree was trimmed and already had presents neatly wrapped underneath for the kids.

Everything was going great until I awoke in the middle of that first night with a terrible cough. The cough and congestion were so bad that my mother called the doctor for a house visit. (Yes, back in 1954 doctors made house calls!) After examining me, the doctor turned to my mother and said, "This baby is very sick. I think you should bring him back to the orphanage and get another one."

Bring another baby back? My parents were thrust back into the state of anxiety associated with my sister's adoption. It wasn't a good time. They were so thankful that the agency had cleared them this time because, between the finalization of Helen's adoption and my arrival, my father had suffered a terrible accident at work that resulted in the loss of his right arm. My parents were afraid the adoption agency would consider his disability as a deterrent to their ability to parent and would refuse their application for a second child.

Matty worked in a paper factory. Part of his job involved loading reels of paper onto a conveyor

belt that would be threaded through the cutting
and folding machine. When in operation, a huge
blade would cut the paper into sections that were
then folded to make paper napkins. Matty wasn't
done threading the paper, but the operator thought
he was finished and fired up the machine before
my father could avoid the blade. His right arm was
severed just above the elbow.

Matty worked hard to rehabilitate himself.
He learned to write with his left hand and how to
dress and drive a car with one arm. Not only did
he figure out how to accomplish everyday tasks,
he also took on additional projects fixing things
around the house. It was amazing to watch how
well he adapted to his situation. Still, Matty and
Emily were afraid the agency would not want to
place a baby in a home that had a disabled parent.

My mother also felt that the odds were against
me.

"I don't know," she told the doctor. "This kid
already has two strikes against him: He has no
family, he's sick…We'll keep him."

So they battled through my illness right along

with me. The nights were the worst. I would wake up short of breath and in the full episode of an asthma attack. My father would sit with me, rubbing my chest with Vick's Vapor-Rub, refilling the vaporizer with water, and rubbing my back to calm me down. It seemed I was always sick around Christmas time. I remember having to stay on the couch and rest while my cousins played with the new toys I hadn't even touched yet. What could be worse for a young child on Christmas day?

When I was six, my parents took me to see an allergist. Back in the late '50s allergy tests were conducted in a very simple fashion. The patient would hold out his or her forearm and the nurse would prick the skin, creating long rows filled with all kinds of samples for things like trees, grass, and foods. I had more than a hundred pricks in each arm and sat there for over an hour waiting to see if any of the pricks produced a reaction.

My results indicated allergies to twenty-four different things…oranges, chocolate, some fruits, various kinds of rag weeds, grass, and trees. I thought I would never see the outdoors again! But the biggest revelation on the list, under the category of trees, was evergreens. I was allergic to Christmas trees!

My father's reaction to the news was both scary and comical. We arrived home and he blurted to my mother, "This kid's allergic to trees! He's been around this damn Christmas tree every year. It's no wonder he's always sick around the holidays."

He grabbed the tree with the bulbs and tinsel still intact and—with his one good arm—wrestled it through the doorway, hauled it down the front steps, and threw it to the curb. Watching from the window, I could see how angry he was and thought I might be next! But my parents dealt with my condition, and I give them a lot of credit because I was obviously more trouble than they'd bargained for!

And as I grew older, I added to their parenting stress. I remember my father looking down at me, shaking his head and asking, "Who is this kid?" because I not only battled with allergies, I had asthma and ran high fevers while my sister remained prim and pretty with no issues at all. When I wasn't sick, I found other ways to get hurt.

I was eight when a sheet of plywood that was

leaned up against a wall in the garage fell on my head sending a nail into my skull and me to the emergency room. At nine, I was balancing on the iron bannister at the top of the staircase that led to our front door when one foot slipped out from under me. I came crashing down on that bannister groin first and had the wind knocked out of me. At nine-and-a-half, I was playing on the steps of a neighborhood nursing home when I missed a step and went head over heels before landing head-first on the concrete sidewalk below. A passerby came rushing to my rescue and carried me home for another trip to the emergency room. At ten, I took an apple in the eye while friends and I were playing in an orchard. Just as I was about to hurl a rotten apple at a buddy, another friend's apple came speeding toward my head and hit me square in the eye.

I was ten-and-a-half when I lit our house on fire. Like I said, more trouble than they bargained for.

The incident happened on a day when I was staying home from school because I was sick (again). I was bored, so my mother tucked me into my parents' bed so that I could watch cartoons on the TV in their bedroom. But I was still bored and started playing with my little plastic army men. Then, I had a great idea. Lining the plastic soldiers up in a row on the floor by the bed, I threaded a piece of string through their legs then grabbed a pack of matches off my mother's night stand. I lit the string to simulate a time-bomb fuse that would blow each man up as the flame traveled the length of the string. Unfortunately, the string wouldn't stay lit. So I kept lighting matches and throwing the dead matches on the bed. All of a sudden I looked up and saw a huge flame coming out of the middle of the mattress. I panicked!

Running to the bathroom, I filled a large glass with water, then ran back to the bedroom and threw the water on a flame that was now almost touching the ceiling. The fire violently hissed when the water hit it, scaring the crap out of me. I ran downstairs where my mother was sleeping on the couch. A big parent rule in our house was "Don't wake me when I'm sleeping," so at first I whispered,

"Mom! Mom!" Then I yelled. When my mother awoke, smoke was already billowing down the staircase. She jumped and ran toward the stairs. As she climbed up the staircase past me, I crouched for protection, thinking she was going to give me a good spanking. "Don't hit me! Don't hit me!" I pleaded. But there was no time for that, the house was on fire!

After making it to the top of the stairs and seeing the magnitude of the fire, she came back down, grabbed me by the hand and pulled me into the kitchen where she called the fire department.

Fire trucks came racing down both sides of the one-way street. All the neighbors came out to watch. I remember standing a few stoops away in my pajamas, watching the fire fighters and good neighbors trying to help. My mother was crying. What was wrong with me? I wondered.

I thought for sure I was going to get the beating of my life when my father came home. But, instead, he talked to me calmly, trying to make some sense of it. I had no answers. I felt horrible. The inside rooms of the house were destroyed, and we had to live with my aunt and uncle for months while my father and uncles spent nights and weekends repairing the damage. The firefighters had banged out the whole back wall in my parents' bedroom to be able to throw the furniture out onto the backyard patio. There was smoke damage everywhere. Toys melted from the heat. The army men were all goners, and it was, indeed, like a war zone.

Accidents had become part of my existence. My uncle Sal used to say, "Well, we know two things about Charles: He's going to be sick, and he's going to get hurt!"

Hey, Look!
I Can Play This Thing Too!

WHILE I BEGAN TO DEVELOP an interest in music when I was eight, I quickly realized that I had an ear for music when I was ten.

My parents bought my sister a brand new piano and she took lessons every week. They asked me if I wanted to take lessons as well, but I thought about my excruciating guitar lessons and quickly said no.

Instead of lessons, I began experimenting on my own with this new instrument in our house. I discovered that I could play songs by listening to the record and then translating what I heard into basic notes and chords on the piano. I think it killed my sister because she relied so heavily on sheet music to play, and while I couldn't read any of those notes in her music books, I could play those songs she was playing, by ear. My favorite way to get under her skin with some sibling rivalry was to mimic what she was playing right after she was done practicing. I would wait for her to finish and as soon as she put the lesson books back inside the piano bench, I would hop on the piano and begin to play something close to what she had been playing. It killed her! I loved it!

---

*I felt accepted. Here was something that
my family truly seemed proud of!*

The Four Seasons, Elvis Presley, and Nat King Cole were all favorites of mine, but when the Beatles came out with "She Loves You" and "I Saw Her Standing There," I had completely caught the bug along with the rest of America's youth. And while all of my cousins and my sister were enthralled by the Beatles, I was the only one who took the time to figure out what they were playing and take note of the harmonies they were singing. When we would sit around the record player with our cousins singing songs on the *Meet the Beatles* album, I would attempt to assign harmony parts to each cousin. But all they wanted to do was sing along to the record, and I was becoming a nuisance to them. They didn't want to learn the harmony parts, but that's okay; they weren't doing it right anyway. I began to sing around the house without any reservation or inhibition.

My grandfather and my father appreciated my talent and encouraged me by putting me in front of the family during gatherings and parties. Singing was the first thing I can remember doing that made my parents seem truly proud. Unlike playing the guitar and getting a sympathetic compliment, I could tell that everyone really enjoyed my singing.

It was through music that I finally felt connected and accepted. My father used to bring home new albums for me to listen to; Sinatra, Bing Crosby, and others. I remember watching a television variety show with my father one night and saw how impressed he was with Sammy Davis, Jr. In this musical special, Sammy Davis was singing, then went over to the drums and started playing, then hopped over to the brass section and grabbed one of the horns. My father's reaction made such an impression on me. He sat there in joy and amazement and said, "Now that's an entertainer."

It wasn't until many years later that I realized how much of a profound effect that moment had had on me. It was the only time I saw my father completely in awe. In the course of my life I taught myself guitar and piano. I took some tap and jazz dance lessons and a few voice lessons. I even enrolled in some NYC acting classes. Years later I realized I was trying to get good at all these things because of that one impressionable moment with my father, watching Sammy Davis, Jr. After my father died, I immersed myself in music.

Music became an outlet for me and I joined a band in the sixth grade. Everyone else in the band had electric guitars and I only had my acoustic guitar. When we played, the electric guitars completely drowned me out. My parents made it clear that because I quit taking lessons I would not be getting an electric guitar any time soon. I thought I was going to be left out of the band until I saw the Rolling Stones and realized I could still be part of the band without playing an instrument. "Hey, I'll sing like that guy in the Rolling Stones!" I thought. So I became the lead singer with a second-hand mic. My friends and I mostly just practiced together, but we did manage to play a few gigs at St. Barnabas school functions. When some of the older kids in school who had a more established band asked me to join them, I gained even more confidence in my talent and abilities.

⌒

Life changed forever in November 1965 when my father was diagnosed with lung cancer. It quickly spread to his brain, and on December 7 of that same year, he died at the age of forty-eight. I was eleven. It was a tough time for the family. As an adopted child, I had now lost two fathers.

Matty, my adoptive father

Everyone loved my adoptive father, Matty, including our family, our neighbors, people at his job, members of the Knights of Columbus, and people at our church. He was someone I admired. To this day, I feel cheated out of what would have been a great relationship.

Me with Dad at Uncle Joe's

One of my fondest memories during our brief time together was when we built a bird house. It was a Cub Scout project. I took a keen notice of how he was able to prop the wood up with his right stump and hammer as a lefty. He was a special man who I think of every day. I feel cheated that my father died so young. While he always seemed a bit hard-nosed and straight laced, I knew he was proud of certain things I could do, like sing, play guitar, and

Matty

play baseball. I often think of how he would have felt seeing me in the high school talent shows or in some of the theatre work I was involved in. After a regional performance of *Godspell* in 1976, I had come from backstage out into the house to meet up with my wife, MaryAnn, and my mother, who were attending. A bunch of patrons surrounded me by the orchestra pit asking me to autograph their program and MaryAnn shared with me later that, seeing this, my mother commented, "His father would have been so proud of him." Hearing those words sent chills down my spine. It was a priceless moment.

But when I really felt cheated by his death was when I married MaryAnn and started having children. I know he would have loved MaryAnn and gotten such a kick out of my kids. And they would have loved him.

MaryAnn, Charlie, Kim, Me, Jessica, and Adam

My father only saw me as a sick kid who always got hurt or in trouble. A kid who hated work. I think my father would have been surprised at how I turned out. After he died the only person I had to look to as a father figure was my uncle John. John was the disciplinarian of the family. We were all terrified of Uncle John! But there was always something about him that led me to believe that he was more caring than most any other relative in our family. To me, it seemed the more he cared, the more strict he became.

In the years after my father died, my mother relied more and more on Uncle John. For a guy who always seemed annoyed, he would drop everything for us and was always helping people as well. While most of us kids feared him, I somehow knew he was instilling fear in us for all the right reasons.

As time went on I learned so much from this man. Oddly enough, he taught me to be a very hard worker. I'm not sure when it happened, but I realized it when I got older and was working three to four jobs at a time to support my family. He was also the person in my life who taught me about integrity and family. He was my "adoptive" father figure and one of the most influential people in my life. I was scared to death of him when I was younger, but grew to love him to death later in life. My wife and children also love him. He and his wife, my aunt Flory, did so much to help me and MaryAnn when we first got married. We were two young kids, still in our teens with a newborn baby, and they were supportive in so many ways. We would not be where we are today without them.

Uncle John at a family reunion, June 2012

Uncle John and Aunt Flory

My mother Emily was never really the same after Matty died. She was so sad and cried a lot. At age eleven, there really wasn't much I could do. I hated when she cried. I felt useless.

But Emily was strong and determined, and despite her own sadness and depressions she alone raised me and my sister to the best of her ability. Emily was tough as nails and I never really appreciated all of her sacrifices until I was old enough to truly understand them. She became both mother and father to us. Of course, I used to call her every Mother's Day, but I also called her every Father's Day. It was our own little inside joke to see who would call whom first, and she got a kick out of that.

With my adoptive mother, Emily

Do You Have a History of ...?

IN 1977, I WAS TWENTY-THREE years old and had two children. Jessica was three and Adam was our newborn. Having kids of my own started me thinking about health issues and my family's medical history. I had been in and out of hospitals since the day I was born, suffering first from asthma and respiratory problems in my early years and then the beginning stages of colon cancer when I hit my late twenties. Luckily, our children had the health of MaryAnn. I don't think my wife ever gets sick!

These chronic illnesses were the cause of complete frustration. Every time I went into a hospital or emergency room, the question of medical history would come up.

"Is there a history of asthma in your family? Does anyone else in your family have a history of stomach problems or ulcers?"

My answer was always, "I don't know."

This black hole in my medical history led me to concerns about the diseases and illnesses that might skip a generation. What if my biological parents had some illness or disease that skipped over me but was looming as a threat to my children? The disadvantage of not being aware of what could potentially be down the road for them was unsettling to me.

I wanted to be prepared, so I decided to do a little ancestral research. Back in 1977, research happened in one place: the library. Adding to this challenge was the fact that all I had to go on was a couple of clues. I started putting together the puzzle from the pieces I had. I remembered the birth certificate my mother showed me, with the last name Cosentino, and I knew I was born in the unwed mothers' section of Misrecordia Hospital. So I decided to look in the phone book for names and numbers under Cosentino.

I was working in the Quality Control Department at American White Cross Labs in New Rochelle, New York. The sales department of our manufacturing plant on Webster Avenue had plenty of phone books from all over: New York, Connecticut, New Jersey, Pennsylvania, and all the places where our vendors and third-party labs were located.

So I started by looking in the Bronx telephone book where Misrecordia Hospital was located, thinking my birth mother might live in that borough of New York City. I found a few Cosentino listings so I picked one and began dialing the number. Before the line started ringing, I quickly hung up, realizing I hadn't prepared myself. What would I say? How would I start this conversation without scaring the person at the other end of the line? It reminded me of that children's book by P. D. Eastman, *Are You My Mother?* where a baby bird goes in search of his mother asking cats and dogs and other animals. Could you imagine? Someone picks up the phone and says "Hello", only to be greeted by someone at the other end inquiring, "Are you my mother?" No, I needed to have a plan!

My mother told me that my birth mother was

unwed and young. Maybe she was sixteen. In doing the math, I figured I would be listening for the voice of a woman currently in her early forties. As I called the first few numbers, my level of anxiety rose with each ring. But there was no answer from any of the first three calls. Back then, voicemail or even answering machines didn't exist, so with each endless ring I would hang up and dial the next number.

On the fourth attempt, I got a hit. The woman who answered sounded frail and much older than forty. I paused to digest the sound of the voice and then asked nervously, "Is this the Cosentino residence?"

"Hello? Yes? Who do you want?" The woman on the other end spoke with an Italian accent. I could tell there was going to be a language barrier if not a hearing issue. She sounded very old. If I wasn't already nervous enough, I was certainly shaking now.

I tried to disguise my nervousness with a friendly upbeat voice, "Hi, I'm looking for Mary Cosentino."

"Mary?" The woman responded as if she couldn't hear or was struggling to understand.

"Yes, Mary," I said, reinforcing that she heard me correctly.

"Okay, you hold on," she shouted. I couldn't believe it. And then adding to my nerves and anxiety, I heard her call out "Mary!"

My heart was pounding. Could it be this easy? I'd only made four phone calls. People spend years and thousands of dollars trying to find their real parents. Was I about to talk to my biological mother? Would she be accepting or would she be annoyed and scared that this deep dark secret of her past had resurfaced?

I heard some commotion at the other end of the line as the receiver was handed to another person, then a voice said very directly, "Hello. Who is this?"

I immediately felt intimidated. But the voice fit the profile. A woman, most likely in her late thirties or early forties asked, "What do you want?" She seemed impatient, almost annoyed.

I tried to collect myself and keep my tone positive and upbeat to counter-balance her intimidating reception. My instincts told me this was not going to be a long conversation, so I tried to get it all out in one breath. "Hi, I'm looking for Mary Cosentino and wondered if you know a Paul Henry Cosentino."

There was a pause. My heart was beating a mile a minute. The pause seemed uncomfortably long, and then she spoke, "Listen, my mother is very ill, and this is not a good time. I don't know what you're looking for. We're very sick here. Good-bye."

She hung up. I stood in silence with the phone still to my ear. I felt as though I just missed getting hit by a bus. Could that have been her? If it was, she didn't sound like she wanted anything to do with me.

But I was too close. Letting that call intimidate me into giving up was not an option.

So I devised a new plan.

I had the address from the phone book listing. I would park on the street and see if I could catch a glimpse of her, looking for any signs of resemblance to me. I knew it was a long shot but I felt I was so close to a major discovery that I should do whatever it took. I would stake out her address in a few days' time.

The next morning, when I got to work, I opened up the *Daily News* and began to read the sections I always read: the headlines, Bill Gallo, the sports section, and Ann Landers, an advice columnist who seemed to have all the answers. Oddly enough, on this day the Ann Landers column was devoted to adoption with two letters from people in search of their real parents.

I never got to the second letter.

The first letter was penned by a girl who mentioned how she found her birth mother and information about her birth father. Neither of them wanted anything to do with her. The mother was rude and didn't appreciate the intrusion on her privacy. The girl was heartbroken and was asking for advice. Ann Landers imparted her wisdom: "Sometimes we fantasize about these situations. We like to think that our parents are living in a beautiful house with a white picket fence in a really nice, upscale neighborhood where they have great jobs. But, in reality, that is not usually the case. More times than not, we find what we don't want to see. A mother working the streets as a prostitute and drug addict, a father on skid row or in jail. Sometimes the adoption is the result of child neglect or abuse. It's better to leave the images of our fantasies intact." Ann's advice was "Don't go looking for your parents unless you are prepared for what you might find."

It was as if I was getting a sign. How coincidental that this article was printed the day after my chilling phone call. More importantly, was I prepared for the worst? The phone call already gave me the sense that this could get confrontational. What if they were horrible people? If they were alcoholics? Would that mean I would be prone to alcoholism?

I thought of how gruff the woman was on the phone a day earlier. If, by chance, it was her, it was clear she didn't want to have anything to do with me.

So at that moment the search was over for me. I was done. I resigned myself to the fact that I was adopted. The information that I have amounts to the only facts I need to know. My real name is Paul Henry Cosentino. I was born in the Bronx and lived in an orphanage for five months before being adopted. My name is now Charles Cornacchio. Done.

And that's the way it stood until a few years later when I felt the urge to see my birth records. My mother didn't remember many details of what she was told about my birth because she and Matty had been so excited that they were bringing a baby home that she hadn't paid much attention. But I wanted to know whatever I could.

I knew that trying to get the birth records in an adoption case was next to impossible at that time, so I devised a scheme. I would pose as a doctor and call the hospital looking for the birth records for "a new patient who I'm treating for asthma."

It was incredibly easy, by today's standards, to just pick up the phone, assume an identity, and have people at the other end of the call believe you. Thankfully, this was before telephones had caller ID, and long before Google Search, otherwise this primitive plan would never have worked!

So I called Misrecordia's Records Administrator, claiming to be a doctor with a new patient.

I asked for his records. "His name is Paul Henry Cosentino. He was born at your hospital in 1954." The Administrator apologized and said that all the records from 1963 and before had been damaged in a fire but that she would check to see if anything was captured on the micro-fiche records that were stored in another facility.

I gave her my "office" number which was actually my home number and told my wife, MaryAnn, that if anyone called she was to first answer with a very professional, "Doctor's office." Fortunately, the call came relatively quickly, and I was able to get a copy of the report the doctor had filed immediately after my birth. It showed my name, weight, time of birth, and some notes that answered a few questions.

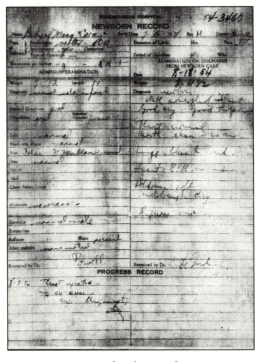

My birth record

By the doctor's notes, it appears that I had respiratory problems at birth. There were several entries noting "heavy mucus and weak breathing." It was somewhat of a victory. I was able to ascertain more information about my birth and confirm that my current respiratory problems were always with me since birth. This examination record in August of 1954 shows how severe my breathing problems were.

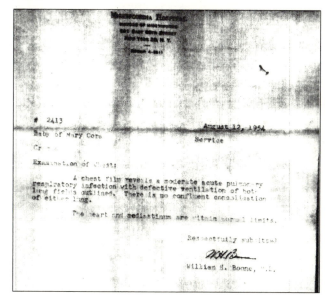

Hard to read, but it basically states:

August 12, 1954

#2413
Baby of Mary Cora
Examination of Chest:

A chest film reveals a moderate acute pulmonary respiratory infection with defective ventilation of both lung fields outlined. There is no confluent consolidation of either lung.

William H. Boone, M.D.

So I felt pretty good that I had made a documented discovery with more history and some new information. After ditching my initial plan, I was happy that I had finally received some satisfaction. And that was to be the end of my search. I had resigned myself to the fact that this was all the information I was going to get … until an amazing course of events happened in 1992—over a decade later!

A String of Coincidences and Circumstances

MARYANN AND I HAD BEEN behind the eight-ball since we were married in 1974. She was seventeen, and I was nineteen. Within three months of saying "I do," we became parents. Although we were still teenagers when our daughter, Jessica, was born, we were about to become responsible adults. The statistical odds were against us from the onset of our marriage. And to test those odds even further, our second child, Adam, was born before I turned twenty-three.

Living with my mother helped with expenses. In 1981, while my children were still small, I left my job at American White Cross Labs for a better job as a Warehouse Group Leader at a start-up telecommunications company called MCI. The company was only two years old, but had just won a divestiture act claim against AT&T and was off and running.

Wedding day 1974, (l. to r.) Russell Sirko, Me, MaryAnn, and MaryAnn's sister Peggy

Being on the ground floor, and having the best boss I ever had—Bob Lewis—made every day an exciting learning experience. I often said that one year at MCI was the equivalent of two or three years at any other company. We were growing so fast, and as a relatively new supervisor in a supply chain logistics environment, I was learning the logistics of logistics. Bob was my mentor, and there was no one better to learn from. Not only was he a logistics genius, he was also extremely supportive of me and my career. Having the type of boss one dreams of having, I began living the dream.

Raises and promotions came quickly because this was a young business that was growing fast. The average age at MCI was twenty-eight. With those raises, coupled with the money I was making as a member of a wedding band on weekends, came the notion that we could afford to buy a house. While we were grateful for my mother's generosity, and how willingly she opened up her small, two-bedroom home with one bathroom, it was time we finally found a place of our own.

We looked for homes about an hour north of where we lived in Westchester County in towns with weird names like Hopewell Junction, Fishkill, and Poughkeepsie. Housing was more affordable the farther north you went and in October of 1982, we settled on a house in Wappinger Falls. The school system seemed decent and the community was friendly enough.

For the first five years I was hardly there. The one hour commute to my job at MCI in Westchester had me out of the house at six thirty in the morning, and I rarely made it home before 7 p.m.

On weekends, and sometimes during the week, I played in a successful wedding band out of Westchester County named Circus.

Our bookings were typically in Westchester, New York City, Long Island, and New Jersey. We played eighty-five gigs a year and the extra income provided a much-needed boost. Unfortunately, it wasn't that conducive for a conventional home life. The band worked every weekend, so I was typically away from home on Friday nights and most Saturdays and Sundays.

Circus: (l. to r.) Gene Moore, Paul Simonetti, Joe Kowalski, and me.

The sixty-mile commute to work got old quick, but the job was good, and the band was great. I excelled at work and received an award for excellent service. Additionally, I was promoted to a management position in the company's distribution center.

This new position came with the responsibility for hiring and managing a staff.

The warehousing industry is known for its high turnover and I soon found myself spending more time than I cared to, interviewing candidates, reciting the company history, going over the benefits package, and providing training. It became very redundant, and, thinking there must be a better way, I started making videos that explained the company history and benefits package so that I wouldn't have to keep repeating myself.

I began writing and directing training videos for our warehouse personnel which led to creating orientation videos for new hires. I had a little experience with film production in high school and had always enjoyed it.

Back in high school I would write, produce, and star in short 8 mm films. When VHS cameras became available to the public in 1978, I was one of the first people on line to purchase a black and white Sony camera and RCA VHS recorder.

Producing training and safety films was just

another way of incorporating the things I liked to do into my work and get paid for it. I loved my job!

Then in 1987, another life-changing moment occurred. MCI was reducing its distribution center network from seven facilities down to just two. The company identified two facilities that would continue to operate, the other five distribution centers would close. The two approved locations were located in Reno, Nevada and Richardson, Texas. Our northeast distribution center in Elmsford, New York along with four other facilities through the Midwest were targeted for closure. About twenty people from our facility were laid off, but I was offered a transfer.

The first offer was for a job in Richardson, Texas, but it was too far and we didn't have any family there. Then, the senior manager in Reno asked me to come out and manage his facility, but I couldn't see raising my children in a gambling environment where prostitution is legal, so I opted for a severance package.

I did a few odd jobs and started a couple of businesses with the money from the severance package and stock options, but startup businesses do not provide a steady enough income.

I began looking for some part-time work to bring in a steady paycheck and in 1988 I saw an ad for a video editor in the employment section of the local newspaper. A local cable TV company was hiring a part-time video editor, and coincidentally, they were building a new facility just up the road from my house.

How fortunate that I had taught myself enough video editing and producing at MCI and was able to parlay that experience into a qualification for this position. A perfect fit, and an easy commute!

I started in January of 1989. It was less than thirty hours a week, and the pay wasn't great, but I really enjoyed being in the TV environment surrounded by the studio cameras, editing machines, and the hustle and bustle of production. On occasion, I was called into the studio as an extra set of hands to help produce the local newscasts. My job was to run the TelePrompTer.

Still, I needed full-time hours, full-time pay,

and I desperately needed health benefits for my family.

So I kept searching the employment ads and came across an ad for an inventory control specialist at Ciba Giegy, a Swiss-owned chemical company with its US headquarters in Westchester County, NY. It seemed like another fortunate coincidence because I had run all of the inventory processes at the MCI distribution center. I had also been responsible for cycle counts, physical inventories, stocking minimum and maximum levels so I figured I could do this job. I convinced myself that the commute wouldn't be that bad. While the position of an inventory specialist was a step down from my MCI management days, I needed the steady income.

The interview process went well and I was hired in May of 1989. I began to reacquaint myself with the long commute. I was thrilled to have a full time job again, but I didn't want to give up my television opportunity, so I managed to work the full-time job at Ciba, keep the band thing going on the weekends, and work nights at the cable company. Everything was back in place. I had a steady income with benefits, a band to make music with on the weekends, and was able to continue delving into this exciting environment of TV News production.

I later realized just how important it was to hang onto the television job because it was instrumental in helping me find out more about my past than I could have ever imagined.

In retrospect, I believe each of the jobs I took and the experiences that came with each all led to a series of coincidences—perhaps even divine intervention—that completely changed my life.

Even the slightest of differences in my career path or life circumstances might have prevented me from the unique discovery that was still ahead: finding my biological mother and learning my complete history.

I am Christian by faith, and believe that all of these incidents and events leading up to this point in time were part of a spiritual orchestration for the reunion of a mother and son. It is clear to me that God had his hand in my life since the day I was conceived.

You'll see what I mean.

Becoming a TV Personality in Six Months

IT WAS MARCH OF 1989 and I had been working part-time at the cable company for three months when a co-worker came into my editing suite holding a piece of paper. "Hey Charlie, did you see this?" It was an internal job posting for a sports anchor for the local news. "You should go for this!"

How exciting that would be, to actually be on TV! It was something I had thought about and, unbeknownst to my peers at the cable company, I had already been somewhat prepared for through my performance background.

You see, back in 1974, through the encouragement of some friends who were part of the drama club at Valhalla High School, I had gotten involved with a summer stock theatre group.

The first stage play I was involved in was the summer of my first year of marriage in 1974. I was a lead dancer in *Hello Dolly*. It was a lot of fun and led to several volunteer community theatre productions, which eventually led to some paid productions with more established and reputable theatre groups in the area. This led to some regional tours, professional dinner theatre productions that came with the perk of a weekly paycheck, and eventually led to earning my Actor's Equity card in 1978.

So being on camera wasn't something I feared. I was the emcee and lead vocalist for my weekend wedding band. I was in front of people every – weekend. I was a performer and I had played sports. So I thought, "Why not?"

I submitted my application and auditioned and three months later I became the first local Sports Anchor for NewsCenter6. My first sports report was on my son Adam's birthday, June 19th.

The position was part-time, which was fortunate because this was just about the time I landed the job at Ciba-Geigy, and it was the Ciba job that provided the salary and benefits that I couldn't give up for the small amount of money the cable company was paying. As long as the sportscaster position was part-time, I could do both.

So there I was, on TV! A pioneer of sorts. I can't remember what my first sports report was about, but it was an exciting time for me and for the department. They finally had a sports anchor, and I was it!

Newscenter6 News Team: Me, Kim Cardinale, David Scholes, Petra Schaeffer, Kevin Garrity, Bob Pucci

Things went along pretty steadily for the first three years. I continued to work for Ciba, leaving my house at 6:30 in the morning to arrive in Westchester by eight, and then leaving work at four in the afternoon, racing up the Taconic State Parkway to make it to the studio by five for a live broadcast at five thirty. After the news, it was time to gather up the equipment and go out to shoot video highlights and collect scores and stories for the next night's broadcast. My weekdays started at six and didn't end until midnight. It was grueling.

On the weekends, I'd shoot afternoon games before rushing to weddings in Long Island, New York, or wherever, and most nights I didn't get home until three in the morning. My days were mostly fourteen- to eighteen-hour days, but I loved what I was doing.

Things were going well at Ciba, and after my first six months, I was promoted from inventory control specialist to inventory supervisor. The following year, I became a distribution specialist. And a few years later, I was recruited by Ciba-Geigy's Corporate Materials Management Department to chair its Transportation Council.

Everything was going great, but out of all the good things happening, it was the sportscasting job that I enjoyed the most. Within six months of taking the position, the cable company assigned me to the Marist College men's basketball games as the color commentator for the live TV broadcasts. Soon to follow, I became the play-by-play announcer for our broadcasting of high school football, basketball, and baseball games.

The simple fact was that this single assignment would change my life, forever.

The sports segment of the news became very popular. It seemed as though everyone was watching. It was a great time to be part of the Hudson Valley sports community.

In March, 1992 I was given an assignment that would eventually put all the puzzle pieces together regarding my adoption.

The Sons of Italy Joe DiMaggio Lodge in Hopewell Junction was hosting a triathlon, and our sports department was assigned to cover it. There really wasn't anything out of the ordinary regarding this assignment. It was like most other events we covered. But in a very short time I would realize that this would be unlike any other event I covered. In fact, it would change my life forever.

Newspaper article of sports coverage

A few weeks after the event was covered and aired on our cable station, the lodge contacted us to attend an appreciation dinner where they planned to present the cable company with a plaque in gratitude for our coverage.

I went as the sports department representative along with our program manager.

The awards ceremony was very nice. The club president made an introductory speech and then called me up to present the plaque of recognition. I approached the podium, smiled as I shook his hand, and we exchanged the plaque. We stood together and posed for pictures. Afterwards, everyone was invited for fingerfood and refreshments and as the attendees started making their way to the refreshments table, the club president came over to me and said, "I gotta tell you. I watch you every night, and you remind me so much of my brother Robert."

This was not unusual for me. People often came up to tell me I reminded them of an uncle, brother, or some celebrity (Tom Selleck, Bill Murray, Tom Hanks, Michael Keaton, and William Shatner to name a few).

I was used to this and brushed it off politely with

a, "Yeah, it's funny how I seem to remind people of someone else."

But he insisted. "No, really. I mean everything about you. The way you look, the way you speak, your mannerisms, everything!" Just then one of his fellow lodge members came into our conversation and pointed at me as he looked at the lodge president and remarked with a big smile, "Hey, it's Robert!" They laughed. Obviously, an inside joke at the Sons of Italy Lodge.

I politely joined in the laughter and then asked the lodge president, "I'm sorry, what was your name again?" He said, "Mike," looking mildly impatient. After all, I had just sat through his presentation and should have remembered his name.

"Mike Cosentino," he said, extending his hand.

My heart almost stopped. His expression told me what my expression must have looked like when I heard that name come from him lips. It was like the effect they use in the movies where the camera closes in on the main character as the background blurs and the sound muffles, and all you hear is heavy breathing and a strong heartbeat. This guy comes up and tells me that I resemble his brother, that we could be related, and then says his last name is Cosentino, the name that I saw on my birth certificate so many years ago!

What was happening here?

I tried to stay calm and make it appear as though I was shrugging it off, but my insides where jumping. Could this be? It was neither the time nor the place to really get into it, so I kept quiet for the rest of the time I was there, but excused myself early. I rushed home, my mind racing, and couldn't wait to tell my wife all about it. MaryAnn asked if I saw a resemblance, but, in all honesty, I really didn't. Mike reminded me of a comedian named Dom Irrera, and I never thought I looked like him.

A few days passed, and while I still thought about that encounter, I wasn't sure how to proceed. By all accounts it seemed like the doorway to my past and answers to all my questions could be right in front of me, but I was hesitant as to whether this was a door I wanted to open. Did I want to meet potential long-lost relatives and risk being disappointed? I tried to let it go, but later that week while I was out covering a local softball game for sports highlights I ran into Mike again.

Apparently he played in the softball league I was covering, and his game followed the one I was assigned to cover. He saw me with my camera in the dugout conducting a couple of interviews, and I could see he was eager to say hello.

When I was done with the interviews he came right up to me, smiled, and said, "Man, I gotta tell you, you are like the spitting image of my brother, Robert. We must be related somehow. You know anybody in New Rochelle?" I told him I used to work in New Rochelle but that my relatives were all from the Bronx. He continued, "Well, I gotta tell you that the resemblance with Robert is uncanny. There's gotta be a relation there somewhere."

I went to the third-base sideline to continue covering the game and asked, "Are you hanging around? We should talk." Mike thought I might be upset by the way he kept bringing the subject up, but I just wanted a more focused conversation without everyone at the park around. As soon as the game ended, I approached him, and we talked along the left field fence while the rest of his team was warming up for the next game. He was on one side, and I was on the other.

And then I said it. I thought I would hold back because I wanted time to digest it, but it just came out. "You know this whole 'related' thing? Well, we might be." He looked inquisitive and confused. Like maybe I was mocking him.

It wasn't until he started to put things together in his own head that Michael remembered. After Robert, there was another baby born, a baby who never came home.

I realized years later that Michael's expression was one of excitement and of nervousness. You see, Michael had already known of the possibility.

Flashback to 1955 when Michael was five years old. As he recollects, he was sitting in the backseat of the family car with his older brother, Louis, and his younger brother, Robert, on either side of him. They were on their way to Lake Placid for their annual summer trip. Mary was in the front passenger seat while Lou, her husband, drove the car. Mary and Lou were arguing, and Michael vividly remembers this ride because of the yelling, the tears, the word "boyfriend," and how adamant Mary was when she said to Lou, "I don't care how long it takes, I'm going to find him."

It wasn't until he started to put things together in his own head that Michael remembered that shortly after Robert was born, there was another baby born, a baby that never came home. Could it be that I was that baby that never came home? Was I the one who Mary and Lou were arguing about? Fast forward to 1990 when Michael sees me on TV and is struck by my resemblance to Robert. That's when he began to wonder, "What if?"

So, as we continued our conversation along the outfield fence, Michael was already beginning to piece things together. "We could be related," I explained. "I was adopted, and my last name was Cosentino." Now Michael was fully engaged.

"Do you have any relatives who live in the city?" I asked.

Michael replied, "No."

"Does your father have a sister named Mary?" I continued questioning.

My rationale here was that if my birth mother's last name was Cosentino and if she wasn't married, she would probably have a new last name now. She was likely the sister of a brother named Cosentino, and could possibly be Mike's aunt. Michael became a little distracted when I asked that question. We were engaged in back and forth questioning up to that point, but then suddenly Michael seemed to disengage a bit. "No," he responded. He paused and then continued, "I have an aunt Amelia but no aunt Mary. Why do you ask?"

"Because I think my mother's name was Mary." Mike became a little flushed and took a step back. He thought I was mocking him, joking with him, but he couldn't fight the facts. The puzzle pieces were beginning to fit. Mary had a baby that never came home. She was crying about finding "him." Here's this guy who looks just like Robert and says his last name was Cosentino and his mother's name was Mary. It was all adding up, and Michael was extremely excited and nervous. But he never let on to me at this point.

I too began to get a little nervous. Frankly, I was afraid that this conversation was actually going to open the door a lot faster than I was ready for.

I had wondered for most of my life, but now that I was approaching the answers to all those questions, I wasn't sure I wanted to know.

Our conversation was cut short as Michael's team was about to take the field.

As I was leaving the complex he shouted, "See ya later, brother!" and laughed with this big smile on his face. I didn't know how to react. I just smiled politely and nodded. As I was leaving the field I turned back, set up my camera, and took some video of him standing out in left field. He knew I was taping, and I could see it was making him uncomfortable.

I went back to the studio and studied the tape, looking for a resemblance and mesmerized by the possibility that I might be looking at my brother! When I got home, I told MaryAnn about my recent encounter with Michael. She was, as I was, stunned. "What are you going to do?" she asked. "Nothing," I said, thinking back to that Ann Landers advice column from so many years ago. "What if it's really them, and I don't like them?"

The next day Michael went to the city clerk's office in New Rochelle, then headed to the town library, looking for clues. Meanwhile, I was simply trying to function at work after a night of lying awake thinking of all the possibilities and the magnitude of this near discovery.

That night at the TV station, as soon as I came off the set, there was a phone call for me. It was Mike's wife. Betty introduced herself and said Mike had told her about our conversation.

"I'm just wondering…" She sounded puzzled. "Did the guys at the lodge put you up to this?" I told her they hadn't, but she continued with a sense of urgency in her voice. "Well I don't know if you know this about him, but Mike's a big kidder, a practical joker, and he's running around New Rochelle and city hall looking for records and stuff. I'm just wondering if the guys from the lodge are trying to get back at him and put you up to this." Once again, I denied that I was part of any practical joke.

"He told me you were asking about an aunt named Mary? What's that all about?" Her voice began to rise with frustration and a sense of interrogation.

"Well," I explained, "I know my mother's name was Mary. She was unwed, so that would mean it was probably her maiden name, and now she's most likely married with a different last name."

There was a pause. Suddenly, the conversation went from increasingly intense, to very quiet. It may have only been about five seconds, but it felt like an eternity.

Finally she spoke softly and said, "That's his mother's name."

Chills ran up my arms. I could feel the hair on the back of my neck standing on end. My heart started pounding as it did that day back at American White Cross Labs when the woman on the phone began to get angry and anxious.

He knew!

When I told Mike that my mother's name was Mary, his body language changed but he didn't reveal that the connection for him was pretty much solidified. Like me, he was being cautious. All I could say to Betty was, "Tell him to call me."

The next day we spoke by phone. Michael is about five years older than I and prides himself on his great memory. He said he remembered when he was between four or five years old, his mother went to the hospital to have a baby, and he and his brothers were sent off to live with aunts and uncles for about four months. He remembers his father taking the boys to a big building with light brick. They would look up to a window and wave at their mother who was waving back.

The hospital I was born in, Misrecordia Hospital, the one I had looked at with new eyes ever since I found out I was born in its "unwed mothers' ward" had light brick and was about eight stories high.

When Mary finally came home, and the family was back together, the baby was not with her. "Could that have been you?" Mike wondered. I told him I was born in 1954 to which he replied that Robert was about a year old at the time of the car ride and was born in 1953, so the timing could have been right. We decided we should get together again. I asked him to bring along any pictures he might have from his childhood, and I would do the same.

I always found it interesting that whenever our family took family photos, I stuck out like a sore thumb. My coloring, my size, everything about me was so different than everyone else in the family. I looked like the kid from down the block who was urged to be included in the group shot by a gracious family member photographer, "Come on, get in there."

Sunday dinner family photo—1962

When Michael and I met again, we began to compare pictures. I immediately saw what he saw. The kids in his pictures and the pictures of me when I was a child looked exactly the same. Coincidentally, both photo albums consisted of the old Polaroid shots, which the camera instantly dispensed, so you could watch the images develop before your eyes. And like the technology that Polariod used to develop its pictures, my connections to my birth family and my history was developing before my eyes.

Louis, Michael, and Robert

These kids had my chubby cheeks, my blue eyes, my big grin...I was a dead ringer for every picture that he had brought with him. In fact, they were all so similar that at the end of our meeting we were getting mixed up as to whose pictures belonged to whom. With the pictures spread out on the table for side-by-side comparisons, Michael sat back with the look of satisfaction as if he just solved an age old mystery. With his hands clasped behind his head and a big grin he was convinced this was it. I was too, but still wanted more proof.

The one thing that puzzled Michael was where the name Paul Henry fit in. Michael said that everyone in the family is named after someone else, and that there was neither a Paul nor a Henry in either family. We agreed that we did all we could do up to this point and the next step was for Michael to talk to his mother. Michael had been holding off because he wanted to make sure we were onto something before getting his mother's hopes up.

Mary lived in an apartment in New Rochelle, and Michael went there every Friday evening to spend time with her and play cards. He said he would ask her about me on his next visit. I nervously waited for the results of this conversation.

In the meantime, as president of the Sons of Italy Joe DiMaggio Lodge, Mike appeared as a guest on one of our cable TV programs called *Meet the Leaders*. He was invited to recap the results of the triathlon organized by the lodge to raise money for a local charity. Knowing when the program was scheduled to air, I turned the channel on at home and called my wife into the living room. I asked her to sit and watch "something" with me. Since MaryAnn had been asking a lot of questions about Michael and our meetings and discussions over the past week, I knew she'd relish the opportunity to see what Mike looked like and sounded like.

When Michael's close-up came on screen, MaryAnn's immediate reaction was, "What are you doing on this show?" I looked at her and just smiled. Then it hit her ... It wasn't me. She gasped, covered her open mouth, and asked, "Is that *him*?" I nodded. MaryAnn got up and walked across the living room floor, putting her nose right up to the screen to get a closer look. The resemblance was uncanny. For the first time in thirty-eight years I experienced a sense of connection and family resemblance. "Oh my God. Oh my God!" was all MaryAnn could say. She said it over and over.

It was a very exciting time.

Friday night arrived and Michael went to visit Mary. She had just had an operation on her knee and was recovering with some hefty pain killers. He brought a VHS copy of my sportscast with him but wanted to ask some questions before breaking the tape out. "Mom," he began, "before we play cards, I want to ask you something." He hoped that the pain medication would make it a little easier for her to open up to him about me.

"I've been thinking back to when we were kids and you went to the hospital to have a baby…" Mary immediately tensed up and started fidgeting. "Why are you bringing that up?" she asked. "I don't want to talk about that." But Michael continued gently, "I've just been wondering, whatever happened to that baby?" There was silence. A long enough pause for tears to begin to well up in Mary's eyes. Michael knew that the secret his mother had

held onto for almost forty years was about to come
to light. "Hold on," she said as she got up from her
chair and hobbled to her bedroom. She returned
with a piece of paper and told Mike it was a note
she had planned on giving to her sons when the time
was right. It would reveal a secret Mary held onto
for thirty-eight years. An account of what happened
back in 1954. She wanted her boys to know they had
another brother.

Mary shared with Michael that although she'd
always planned to tell her sons that they had another
brother, the right moment never seemed to present
itself. In fact, she had written the note just before her
knee surgery with the intention of sharing it with
her sons just in case "anything bad happened" to her
during the procedure.

"I was going to tell you boys about your brother,
but I never knew how to say it. I couldn't tell you
while your father was alive because the baby wasn't
his. But that baby," Mary paused. "He died." Michael
waited a few seconds before pressing, "How do you
know that baby died?"

"Because about two years after he was born I told

your father I was going to go out and look for him,"
she explained. "But your father had already done an
investigation, and he told me then that he found
out the baby died of spinal meningitis."

Interesting how times have changed! Back in
1954, when a husband told his wife something,
more times than not, she automatically believed it.
Michael continued to probe, "Was there a funeral?
Did the baby have a head stone? A name?"

"We never had a funeral but, yes, I did name
him," Mary said. "I named him Paul Henry."

Michael felt chills when he heard his mother
say that name for the very first time. He collected
himself and asked, "Why Paul Henry? Where did
that name come from?"

Mary nodded. "I named him after the nun who
ran the ward I was in, Sister St. Paul, and her assistant, Sister Henry." Tears streamed down her face.
"They took such good care of me." Mary wiped her
eyes then continued, "Sister St. Paul sat with me
after I had the baby. I wanted so badly to bring him
home. He was mine. For three days I held him and
fed him and tried to convince your father to let me

bring him home. But Sister St. Paul convinced me that I would be bringing a baby into a home where he wasn't wanted." Mary was reliving the moment as if she was right back in the hospital. She cried out, "and then they took him from me!" Mary paused to collect herself and fought through the tears as she continued, "The days after that were empty. I was so sad for what I had done and that I had to give my baby away. The Sisters helped me get through that."

Michael had so many questions and Mary did her best to answer them. "Your father made me give him up," Mary told him. "He said, 'If you bring that baby home, I'm going to take the boys and leave you out on the street.'"

I can't imagine what that was like for Mary. I only know that the world was a much different place and that women didn't have the options and independence that they have today. In retrospect, I don't even want to imagine how different my life would have been if Mary had been able to get her way and brought me into what would surely have been a hostile environment. Her husband would have resented me and pitted the other three boys against me. I know my life would have been very different than the way it turned out. Additionally, imagine the turmoil it would have caused me, my adopted parents, and even my extended family if, in fact, Mary had searched me out and found me. I know it would have been confusing and messy, so I'm glad things happened the way they did.

Eventually, Michael pulled out the VHS tape and began to play it for Mary. It contained footage of me anchoring the sports report for the evening news. Even Mary thought I was her son Robert at first. "What's Robert doing on TV?" she wanted to know. "That's not Robert, Mom." Michael spoke quietly, "That's him. That's that baby." Mary seemed overwhelmed, "It can't be him. My baby died."

"Nope," Mike assured her. "He's alive. I met him, and he told me his birth name was Cosentino, and he knows that his mother's name is Mary. When he was adopted they changed his name to Charles."

Mary was stunned.

"My baby is alive?" she asked as the realization brought her to tears.

Michael moved over to sit next to her. Slowly, he filled her in on our chance meeting and all the conversations we had had up to this point.

Later that night, Michael called my house and spoke to MaryAnn. "Tell Charlie we hit a home run." He beamed. "Have him call me."

As soon as I got home, I went straight to the phone in the kitchen. Michael confirmed that his mother confessed to having a son that she had to give up and that she had named him Paul Henry.

"So that's it, right?" Michael asked, hoping that he garnered enough proof for me to finally admit that we were brothers.

I wanted to agree but still needed time to digest it. The newest information he offered about being named after the nuns at the hospital was worth investigating.

So I called Misrecordia Hospital. I worked my way through various departments until I had the head of administration on the line. I didn't know where to start but began by conveying that I was an adoptee and that I was fully aware of the privacy acts that prevented her from giving out any information. I explained that I thought my birth family had found me and that I just needed some basic information to confirm it. Before I could ask any questions, the administrator had one for me. "How do you know you were born here?" I told her that my adoptive mother had given me the hospital name and, while I didn't tell the administrator how I'd posed as a doctor to get them, I explained that I had seen medical records that included the name "Mary" in the parent's section of the document followed by the name "Cora" in quotes.

The administrator seemed sympathetic. The mention of the name "Cora" was key for her. "Oh yes," she began, "that was a code we used to protect the identity of the mother. We would take the first letter of the person's last name and make a different first name that started with that letter. So, okay, looks like you were born here. And what do you want to know, because I can't tell you much about the case." I could tell she was on my side and would try and do as much as she was allowed.

"My birth mother said she named me after the nun who ran the ward at that time," I told her.

She asked for my birth year. When I told her I was born in 1954, she immediately responded with, "That would have been Sister St. Paul."

I was silent.

"She ran the ward up until she died last year."

Knowing what the answer to the next question was going to be but still needed to ask, "Did she have an assistant?"

"Yes, that would be Sister Henry."

And that was it. All the pieces to the puzzle were fitting together. It was overwhelming to digest. I had found my birth mother! Suddenly I had a history. Moments earlier my history amounted to the footprint of my last step, and now I had a history that ran miles behind me.

When it comes down to it, I wasn't even looking for her, but the circumstances and events over the past few weeks revealed answers to a thirty-eight-year mystery. How many adopted people can say that? It was a monumental moment. But there was still more to come.

⁓

More importantly, I was about to have an advantage that most adopted children never get. I had a clear vision of what every adopted child wonders: What would my life have been like if my real parents kept me?

Now I knew! I could see what my life would have been like had my mother got her way and kept me, as opposed to what my life actually turned out to be.

Had Mary kept me, I would have been fighting for my life every day, living with a father who resented me and three brothers he would have surely turned against me. I would have shared one bedroom with three other brothers, as the Cosentinos lived in a two bedroom apartment in New Rochelle and in Harrison.

I most likely would not have had the encouragement and support I received from my adopted family. Not because the Cosentino's were bad people, but because of the tainted circumstances of my birth.

The way it happened turned out much better because I can now enjoy my brothers without all the sibling rivalry baggage that we might have built up over the years.

Do You Want to Meet Her?

I CALLED MICHAEL AND TOLD him about my conversation with the hospital administrator, and he presented the question I'd been afraid to ask myself.

"Do you want to meet Mary?"

Every nerve in my body responded.

"Does she want to see me?" I managed.

Michael was honest. "I don't know," he said. "But, I'll ask her."

Mary was hesitant. What if I resented her for giving me up? Maybe I would be angry. But Michael did a good job of convincing Mary that I simply wanted to meet her to learn more about my past.

I wanted so badly to tell my mother, Emily. Emily was a tough woman but could also be very fragile. I didn't want her to think that I was looking for my birth mother because there was something lacking in our relationship. Emily was both mother and father to me for most of my life. After my father died, Emily never married. I don't even think she ever went on a date. Her focus was on me and my adopted sister, Helen.

I'm sure Emily questioned herself as most parents do. "Am I giving these kids enough? Am I a good enough parent on my own?" The one thing that I didn't want to happen was to give Emily any reason to doubt herself. She'd done an excellent job. But I needed to meet Mary first; then I could share the exciting news with my mother.

Michael arranged for me to meet Mary on a Sunday in May of 1992. Coincidentally, it was Mother's Day.

I bought flowers and followed Michael down to New Rochelle. We pulled into the parking lot at Mary's apartment building and walked into the lobby together. Michael just kept looking at me. His stare was uncomfortable. We laughed about it.

"Stop looking at me!" I said, nervously.

But he couldn't stop himself. It was a monumental moment for Michael, as well. Ever since he realized that there was another baby out there he wondered if he would ever meet him. So it was as big a moment for Michael as it was for me.

We walked into the elevator. He was looking at me. He pushed the button to Mary's floor and kept looking at me. The elevator engaged. Michael watched my face. The elevator stopped, and the doors opened. I exited and took a deep breath. The walk down the hallway to Mary's door seemed to be looming from some great distance.

When we finally approached the door, Michael was smiling. He was enjoying this, seeing how nervous I was with anticipation. "Are you ready?" he asked with his hand on the doorknob. I took another deep breath and nodded.

I was about to experience the most significant moment in my life. This door was not only the entrance to Mary's apartment, but the portal to all the answers and the history that had eluded me for thirty-eight years. A lifetime of questions were about to be answered. Michael twisted the knob, and the door opened.

I followed my brother down a short, narrow hallway that led to a living room, and there she was: my birth mother, Mary. All five-foot-nothing of her. Her hair, all done up as if she'd been to a beauty parlor, was dyed a color somewhere between orange and yellow. She was obviously Italian and her light blue eyes were very similar to my own. Mary used the walker she'd been issued after her knee surgery to stand up. I said, "Hello," and handed her the flowers. She began to cry and hugged me until tears welled up in my eyes, too.

We stood there for what seemed an eternity just holding each other. Mary's words were muffled by my embrace, but I could hear her saying over and over, "I'm sorry. I'm so sorry."

I was still holding back my tears and when we released our embrace. I tried to reassure her. "There's nothing to be sorry about. Everything worked out fine."

We both composed ourselves and sat in the

living room. Mary commented on my eyes. "I remember when you were born that your eyes were so blue," she said, dabbing at her matching set with a tissue. "Everyone talked about what a beautiful baby you were." She looked me over as if inspecting every facet and feature of my face. She paused, and through her tears, added, "It was so hard for me to give you up."

She spoke so fast! Like she couldn't get the words out fast enough. She was extremely excited and nervous.

Mary, 1992

We talked about everything. How I came to be, about my birth father, and all the relatives I have that are living in Mamaroneck, the next town over from New Rochelle. I brought a photo album to show her pictures of me growing up, and she compared them with her own photo album holding plenty more photos of people who looked like me!

Here's what I learned. At the time I was born, Mary was the mother of three boys: Louis, Michael, and Robert. Mary was having an affair with a man from the neighborhood. She had just given birth to Robert and, before she had sex with her husband, Louis Sr., she was pregnant again. This was not the immaculate conception of the new millennium, so there was never any denying that Mary was having an affair.

This affair was with a man named Robert Harris. Robert worked for Neptune Movers, a popular moving company in New Rochelle. He, his wife, June, and Mary and Louis Cosentino were all part of a group of neighbors who gathered at each other's homes to play bridge on Friday nights.

On bridge night, Bob Harris would bring his

guitar and play and sing as part of the night's enter-tainment. Mary loved country music, and Bob obliged her by playing and singing a few country tunes. "I fell in love with him," Mary recalled. "He was so handsome, and when he sang... well, I think all the women fell in love a little bit."

It's unclear if the affair started long before I was born, but in a subsequent meeting I had with Bob's wife, June Harris told me that she believed Mary's middle son, Robert, was Bob's child as well.

In this conversation with my mother there was one revelation after another. I was trying to remember it all word for word and wished I had brought a tape recorder.

One of the questions in my life was answered. My gravitation to music, and my ability to play and sing without any training had always puzzled me. But here was the answer. Bob Harris sang and played guitar, so I'm assuming my musical ability is genetic.

Mary confided that when Louis found out she was pregnant, he demanded that Mary get rid of the baby and threatened to take their three boys and leave her on the street if she didn't. So, to save embarrassment and shame, Mary was packed up and sent to Misrecordia Hospital while the three boys were shipped to various relatives' houses until the ordeal was over.

This is the memory that Michael had shared. He'd remembered that the boys were split up for a time, and that it was a while before they could go back home. Mary told me about her hospital stay and how the nurses and nuns were so caring and kind. She recounted the day I was born and how she held me in her arms and debated whether to fight for her right to keep me. Mary did keep me for three days while she tried to convince her husband to let her take me home. She said that it was Sister St. Paul who really convinced her to give me up for adoption. It was Sister St. Paul who asked, "What kind of life will this baby have if you bring him into a home where he's not wanted?"

And Sister St. Paul was right. How different a life I would have had if Mary had brought me home. A constant reminder of Mary's infidelity. If I survived that upbringing, I certainly would have been a totally different person. Instead, I was put in the Catholic Home Bureau for Dependent Children on Twenty-Second Street in New York to wait for a family to take me home.

Mary shared what Michael had told me about her wanting to look for me shortly after she came home, and how she was told that I had died. There was so much information, and I was absorbing it like a sponge. All the facts and stories. Suddenly, everything made sense. It was exhilarating, and then, in a quiet moment while Mary was in the bathroom, something else occurred to me, something that, once again, pointed to the many coincidences that led up to this visit.

While Mary was in the other room, I got up from the sofa and started walking around the apartment, looking at pictures staged around the living room. I went to the window to look down at her view from the fourth floor … and there it was, a softball field I remember playing on that I hadn't seen in fifteen years and probably would never have seen had I not worked for American White Cross Labs in New Rochelle back in 1977 when the company formed a softball team.

I'll never forget the first time we played there. I could not believe the field layout. The field pointed toward a huge apartment building that was planted in left field. When we approached the field I immediately commented on the close proximity of the building and asked, "What happens when we break a window?" I put my cleats on and ran out to my position in left center field. I remember trying to get a feel for tracking a fly ball and holding my open hand out to feel for the wall before I ran into the building. It hit me that I was standing in the building I had been so concerned about back then. I was playing softball right under my birth mother's nose and never knew it until now.

Of course, I had no idea my birth mother lived here then, or that she might even have seen me if she happened to look out the window while we were playing. All I was thinking about at that time was "what a stupid place to put a building."

Our visit lasted a couple of hours. I asked if I could bring my family to meet her to which Mary gladly accepted. When I arrived back home I gathered MaryAnn, Jessica, Adam, and Kim to share the experience of my meeting with Mary. Weeks later, I brought my family down to meet her. Mary loved cooking dinner and we would sit and talk, having a few laughs and nice visits.

There was, however, one particular visit where things didn't go so well. Mary shared something she hadn't told me and I wished she never did; especially in mixed company with my wife and children as her audience.

Sitting at the dinner table with my kids mesmerized and excited by all the stories of the old neighborhood and how their father came to be was suddenly overshadowed when Mary decided to share something very sensitive and intimate. I think she was just filling the kids in on what was happening at the time and didn't really see much significance in it, but it hit me with such surprise and sadness.

Mary was explaining her surprise and fear when she realized she was pregnant. She knew that all of her secret rendezvous would be uncovered. Mary was at a loss about what to do for fear of the shame from other neighbors and the anger of her husband.

She took drastic measures. And while we sat at the table, Mary shared the story of how both she and the wife of the man she was having an affair with, tried to abort me with concoctions of mixed chemicals that Mary would drink during the early stages of her pregnancy. She couldn't have this baby, but a back-alley abortion was not an option. Together they mixed different solutions of cleaning products and other household chemical concoctions in the hopes that this pregnancy would go away.

Could this be why I have had respiratory and digestive problems throughout my life? Hard to say, I guess, but it confirms to me that I was meant to be born. I survived the chemical onslaught and whatever else these two women attempted in an effort to extinguish the life inside Mary. God had been protecting me. There was a reason I was born and, today when I look at my family, I can give you thirteen of them: four beautiful children, eight beautiful grandchildren, and one beautiful wife.

Aside from being stunned that Mary would share such sensitive and personal information with my children, all I could think about was how lucky for me that those chemicals didn't cause a more serious health issue or brain damage. Could this explain the doctor's notes about severe mucus and breathing problems recorded in my birth records? Could this explain why I was so sick when the Cornacchios brought me home? Could it explain why I had been so sick throughout my life?

I had been hospitalized several times for severe asthma attacks, missed a lot of school, and, in my late thirties, had a major colonectomy with the removal of my entire lower intestine. It was a three-operation process that went wrong and caused me to need a fourth operation in a span of nine months. I lost over sixty pounds from the ordeal, going from the 190s to the 130s. All the while, doctors kept asking, "Is there a history of ulcers or colitis in your family?"

I'm grateful my illnesses never stopped me from doing the things I loved to do. I still played baseball and football. I sang in my band but it wasn't always easy while I was having major respiratory problems. At times it had gotten so bad that I had to bring a nebulizer kit to the gig, and find a quiet, private place to use it during breaks, just to get through the job. I didn't want to lose the wedding band gig because the money was so good and, with four kids, we needed every bit of it.

I worked hard at trying not to appear sickly. There were a couple of times that I headed straight from gigs to the emergency room for a shot of epinephrine to prevent the onslaught of a full-blown asthma attack. Those were tough times. During my sportscaster days I lost a lot of weight due to internal bleeding from ulcerative colitis. I tried my best to hide the illness, but if you know someone who has ulcerative colitis then you know how difficult it can be to be out in the middle of a field with no bathroom in site. Eventually I was forced to take medical leave to have the series of operations.

Because Mary would say whatever was on her mind, and after the bombshell from that dinner, I decided to stop bringing the kids with me for visits. Most of the time she said funny stuff, but you just never knew when something unexpected would come out. I thought it best that the kids didn't have that kind of exposure.

So, hearing about my history was not only exhilarating and interesting, it could also be quite painful.

But at least now I had answers! Not *all* the answers, but a good portion of my life-long puzzle was in place with the exception of one missing piece. I had to learn about my birth father's medical past to complete my medical history. To do this, I needed to talk with June Harris to find out if Bob had any illnesses.

Mary said that she didn't talk to Bob or see him again after I was born. Once the affair was out in the open, the relationship ended and everyone stayed to themselves. But to their credit, even in 1954 when divorces were not easily granted, the broken vows were still honored with commitment, and they all stayed married. A true testament to a great generation.

Mary recalled that she saw Bob's obituary in the newspaper a few months before our meeting. I looked it up in the *New Rochelle Standard Star* and there it was. Robert Harris, age 74, died in March of 1992. So now, with this information from Mary, I was ready to complete the puzzle and that meant tracking down Robert Harris's wife, June Harris.

June Harris obviously knew of the affair but had just lost her husband, and I wanted to be sensitive about bringing the subject up again. Getting to this meeting would require a delicate balance.

Mary didn't have June's contact information, but when I pulled Robert Harris's obituary from the newspaper, I noted the funeral home where his wake had been.

I called the funeral parlor, and, in my best "old man character voice" said, "Hi, I just saw in the paper that a friend of mine died, Bob Harris."

I wasn't sure if the man at the funeral home was buying it, but I kept at it.

"I was out of the country and just found out. Such a shame." I paused, hoping for a little buy-in, but this guy wasn't talking.

"Anyway, I would like to send a sympathy card or some flowers to his wife, June."

I was thinking that dropping June's name would make me sound legit, but, I realized later, it was printed in the obituary.

"I don't have her address and wondered if you could provide it?" I continued.

There was an uncomfortable pause, then a simple, "Hold on."

I thought, "Wow! I'm getting pretty good at this! First the hospital birth records and now these guys!"

When he came back to the phone, the man's tone was direct. "Send whatever you're going to send to us here at the funeral home, and we'll make sure she gets it."

I could tell by his tone that he was trying to call my bluff.

I decided to buy a mass card and slip a note inside so only June would see it. I wrote that I was sorry to hear of her loss and explained who I was. I let her know that I had children of my own and that I wanted to provide them with the information they needed to have complete medical histories. I questioned if Bob had any illnesses that might skip a generation because this could impact my children's health. I kept the focus on my children, but, of course, I was also curious to know as much as I could about my biological father.

I included my phone number, mailed the card to the funeral home, and, within two days, I received a phone call.

I was pulling into the driveway, coming home from work, when MaryAnn came outside to meet me. As I got out of the car she said in a very excited and nervous voice, "Guess who just called?"

At the time, it could have been any one of a number of creditors, and June was not the first person to come to mind. "Who?" I asked.

"June Harris!" MaryAnn said with anticipation. "She wants you to call her!" I was shocked. Not only did that card get to her quickly, but June was quick to call. I hadn't expected her to be so receptive to the notion of speaking with me. I went into the house and immediately dialed the number Maryann had scribbled on the back of an electric bill envelope. My nerves started their now familiar rise. This was becoming an emotional rollercoaster ride!

June answered and even sounded happy to hear

from me. "Oh, you poor thing," she began. "I got your letter and wanted to call you right away because I know you are worried about your children." Relief settled my nerves. She was sincere and welcoming. I asked if I could meet with her, and she gave me her address. A few days later, I drove to her home in New Rochelle.

It was a tough meeting for a number of reasons. Since Bob had just died, asking questions about him and the affair could only bring back memories of a bad time in their lives. It was touchy. I would tread lightly.

We sat in the living room, and June had a couple of pictures of my birth father. Amazing! Immediately, without either of us saying a word, another of my many questions was answered. My son Adam is the only one of four children who doesn't resemble me or MaryAnn, at least to the degree of his siblings. That's because he looks like Robert Harris.

June told me about the affair. She cried and paused from time to time to collect herself. It was uncomfortable because while I didn't want to cause her pain, I did want to make the most of this rare opportunity to get her side of my story.

June described Mary as a "harlot." She said, "We were friends, but that Mary was sneaky." I could tell she was holding back from saying what she really felt but still had great animosity toward Mary and the whole situation, even after all these years.

"And the nerve of that woman," she continued, "naming that other boy after my Bob." Come to think of it, it was coincidental that my newly discovered brother, just twelve months older than me, was named Robert. This is what led me to believe that the affair between Bob Harris and Mary was going on long before I was conceived.

June continued to recollect, "Mary would come over to my house and ask if she could use my bathroom," she stated with a tone of suspicion. "Every time she came over to my place she needed to use the bathroom. One day I said to her, 'Mary, your house is right down the street. Why can't you use your own bathroom?'" June stopped, and began to sob.

I liked June. What she must have felt going through this whole ordeal thirty-eight years ago, and the loss she was going through at this moment, three months after losing her husband Bob to cancer at age seventy-four.

June composed herself and continued, "So that's how she communicated with my Bob! She was leaving notes. Hiding them under the sink in the bathroom for Bob to find when he came home from work! I know this because I found one that fell to the floor!"

As she reflected on these events, she had dismissed all the words said and odd behavior at the time, but now in hindsight she realized they were signs of trouble. I could tell that June was disappointed. She wished that she'd figured out the truth about Mary and Bob sooner.

Of course, in the 1950s there was no texting, no cell phones, and no e-mail. They couldn't call each other's house phones, so Mary and Bob got a little inventive.

June told me that Bob was a great athlete and an excellent swimmer. He had won races and

Bob Harris

earned medals. Since I was athletic, I considered this another correlation to Bob's genes.

I later found out that my brother Robert was also an athlete. At five-feet eight-inches tall, he was the star quarterback on the football team and a star pitcher on the high school baseball team, earning him a scholarship to Iona Prep. Robert was the only one in his family that showed such a high degree of athleticism. Michael was interested in sports and a good baseball and softball player, but not to the level of Robert.

June and Robert Harris had two children. Mary seemed to think they were adopted because she remembers that June could not have children. I never asked.

We talked for an hour or so before June's daughter came home, and suddenly the mood and tone of conversation seemed to change.

I was introduced to the Harris's daughter and greeted with a very cold *When are you leaving* sort of hello and handshake. She sat at the other side of the room and, though she never said a word to me, she watched me like a hawk. Perhaps this was a daughter being protective of her newly widowed mother, but as soon as she entered the room the previously warm and congenial conversation turned into the likes of a cold supervised visit.

It wasn't until recently that a friend suggested that June's daughter probably thought I was looking for an inheritance. I had never thought about that until he mentioned it, but I think this was a daughter trying to spare her mother any further heartbreak. I suddenly felt very inhibited, and thought it best to temper the personal questions that would be uncomfortable in front of an outsider. As far as I knew, this girl didn't know the story or understand my concerns and lifelong questions.

We talked about clinical health concerns and June let my mind at ease with the understanding that Bob was in good shape and didn't suffer from any of the chronic illnesses I had, or any conditions that might skip a generation and hold potential threats to my children's health. I was grateful to hear this.

I thanked June for being so candid with me, conveyed my sympathy for her loss, and left thinking we might meet up again in a few months after she had enough time to get through her grieving process. But we never saw each other again.

The Meeting of the Brothers

THE NEXT STEP IN THIS process was to meet all four of the Cosentino brothers: Louis, Michael, Robert, and Vinny. Vinny was the youngest brother. He was born a few years after I was given up for adoption. Michael set up the meeting at his house by inviting me to his daughter's fourteenth birthday party. The timing was perfect because all the brothers were expected to attend the party.

When Michael told me where he lived, I laughed.

As it turns out, we had been living just a mile from each other in Wappinger Falls for the past ten years and never knew it!

How coincidental that two guys who lived in Westchester County both decided to move sixty miles north, to the exact same area, at around the same time. Now knowing that Michael had moved to Dutchess County in 1981, and we moved there in 1982, it almost seemed odd that we hadn't ever run into each other before that fateful dinner sponsored by Michael's Sons of Italy Lodge.

Michael later shared with me that he used to feel people were looking at him and whispering whenever he was out and about around town. He didn't realize it then, but because of our similarities in appearance, he wondered now if people thought he was the sports guy from TV.

"We would be at a restaurant," Michael explained, "and people would keep glancing over at me. I would look away, but when I looked back, they would still be looking at me and whispering."

Michael said his wife, Betty, used to tease him and say it was wishful thinking.

"But I felt very uncomfortable," Michael added. "Thinking about it now, I just think all these people thought maybe I was you!"

The birthday party was on a rainy Saturday. I was to arrive at three o'clock and could barely wait.

Imagine, first my mother and now brothers!

From left: Vinny, Charles, Mike, Robert, Louis

I'd always wanted a brother, and now I had four! Still, I was apprehensive. I started to feel the anxiety of this monumental moment. Would I like them? Would they like me? I was hoping they weren't jerks. I was hoping they wouldn't think I was a jerk.

To be honest, driving to Michael's house felt surreal. For 38 years of my life I had no past, – and suddenly within a few weeks I met my mother and now I'm about to meet the four brothers I never knew I had. The drive to Michael's house from my house was only one mile, but it felt much longer than that as all these new thoughts and emotions were racing through my head.

It was a damp and wet day. The rain felt like a symbolic cleansing that was washing away all the years of unanswered questions and curiosity. As I pulled up to the house, I could see about twenty people peeking through the curtains of the bay window. When I got out of my car and looked toward the house I planned to put on my best smile, but they all scattered. It was comical, but also unsettling for a number of reasons.

To most people who lived in our Hudson Valley area, I was the TV sports guy.

So here's the TV sports guy walking toward the house and, oh wait . . . he's also a long-lost brother, uncle, or brother-in-law.

Oh yes, this was going to be interesting.

Michael came out to meet me and led me through the garage where he had five folding chairs set up in a semicircle. We walked past the chairs and into a house full of people—all of them trying to look busy as if nothing out of the ordinary was going on.

Then the introductions started. Everything was happening so fast, I didn't know what was going on. Suddenly I'm meeting one of the brothers, – then I'm shaking the hand of someone's mother-in-law, I met another brother, and then I'm meeting nieces and nephews. It was all so confusing.

Once we were done with the introductions, Michael led the brothers out into the garage. We sat down and just looked at each other. Actually I looked at each of them as they were studying me. What I noticed was that we *all* had mustaches. How coincidental and funny is that?

They were all checking out my ears, my mouth, my nose, my eyes, comparing all of my features either to themselves or some Uncle Joey, Uncle Louie, or whatever. There was great excitement in the air.

Everyone was engaged except Louis, who seemed to be going through the motions, but really could not have cared less about this life changing moment.

Keep in mind that Louis was the oldest brother, about seven years my senior. Michael had told me that Louis had always been at odds with Mary and that he rarely had time for any of the brothers.

Michael believes that Louis's indifference stemmed from the fact that he was old enough to remember Mary's affair with Robert Harris and held it against her.

I'm not sure Michael noticed Louis's standoffish demeanor because he was busy playing host at the party. It was a very exciting time for Michael, and he wanted to make sure everyone was comfortable. It struck me how good Michael was at that. He had a great sense of humor and an uncanny ability to diffuse any stressful situation.

Robert, who is just a year older than me, sat in the chair closest to mine. Soft-spoken and reflective, he seemed amused by the whole event. Robert seemed excited, but guarded. He asked me a lot of questions, almost as if he was trying to find out about himself. He played sports. I played sports.

He said, "I hear you play guitar?" I nodded and he smiled. "I used to play guitar in a band in high school." He was the only brother who was musical. Another indication that we might be full brothers.

Vinny, the youngest, was like a kid at Christmas. He was so excited by the whole thing. He kept announcing in astonishment, "I got a new brother! I can't believe it! What are the chances?"

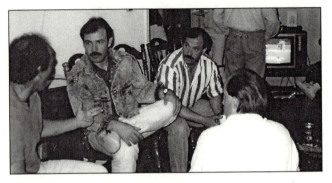

Robert, Me, Michael, and Vinny continuing the conversations during our first meeting. Louis with his back to us, watching the game on TV

I could tell immediately that, being the youngest brother, Vinny was the brunt of all the jokes and that all of his older brothers picked on him as a kid. He seemed used to it, but watching them interact made me wonder how I would have held up if I had been part of this group since birth. It was Vinny who kept talking about family. Family was extremely important to him, and it appeared that he was trying to make up for years of lost time.

The meeting lasted about two hours. It went off as I had hoped it would.

I found them all to be very nice and we began to find excuses to meet up and hang out.

I was invited to graduation and birthday parties. They were invited to birthday parties and weddings.

Michael and me at his son Brian's wedding, 2009

My family has been extended, and I'm very fortunate that it turned out the way it did.

At that time I was playing in a thirty-five-and-older baseball league and arranged to get both Michael and Robert on my team the next season. It was something I was very excited about. Finally having brothers, and playing baseball together! I looked forward to each and every game. It was comical because, with our mustaches and batting helmets on, opposing teams would get confused. If Robert, Michael, and I were separated in the batting lineup, inevitably the pitcher or catcher would claim that our team was batting out of order whenever the second brother got up for the first time in a game. "Hey ump, this guy was just up!" It was hilarious and happened at least five times during the season before people realized we were brothers.

I'm probably closest with my brother Michael, maybe because he was the first one to make the connection and the one who took me to meet Mary. We've been out to dinner with our wives, invited to each other's daughters' and sons' graduations and weddings, and we keep in touch more than I do with my other brothers.

We also live close by and have had several unplanned run-ins at the local Dunkin' Donuts where we catch up on things and share a laugh or two.

Louis died in 2006 from cancer. He was fifty-eight. I learned more about Louis from the other brothers than from Louis himself.

He had a difficult life. As a veteran of the Vietnam War, Louis suffered from post-traumatic stress well after his tour of duty. Fourth of July celebrations were the worst, especially when he first got out of the Army. A surprise firecracker or cherry bomb explosion would send him under the coffee table ducking for cover.

Robert had called me and asked if we could meet privately. Robert shared with me that throughout his life he always had thoughts and concerns that he wasn't really part of his family. He confided that he had these feelings since he was a kid and wondered if we were really full brothers and if Bob Harris was his father too. Robert didn't know about the conversation I had with June Harris when she remarked, "…and the nerve of Mary to name that kid after my Bob." Robert also didn't know that Bob Harris was musically inclined, just as we were. And he didn't know that Bob was athletic, also, as we were.

Was it my place to say? I wasn't sure I should share the similarities or revelations I uncovered for fear that I might just confuse the issue or divide their family a little bit.

But it was disconcerting that Robert seemed bitter. He said he felt I was the one who had the better life.

"You were the lucky one," he professed.

Hearing his stories of what it was like growing up in a family of four boys who all shared the same bedroom, Robert's remark rang true. He said he spent much of his childhood looking after his younger brother Vinny while his mother was out working.

"I remember on more than a few occasions, my mother would take me and Vinny in the car and drive around New Rochelle," he recalled. "She would park outside a bar and have us wait in the car while she went in 'looking for somebody.'"

He tried to make sense of it then, and now, with all of this new information, Robert surmised, "I think she was probably looking for Harris!"

There was something about Robert that made me feel good whenever we were together. It was a definitive kinship that I felt. Probably because I suspected we were actually full brothers. Robert owned a successful fence company and had two boys with his first wife. They divorced and he remarried, having a girl and boy with his current wife, Tammy.

They live in Port Chester, New York.

I thought it best to leave everything up for speculation, but I think we both knew we were full brothers without ever saying it.

⌒

Michael had the personality of an entertainer. He was a comedian. Later, while watching him interact with people in the community it became apparent that Michael was well liked and well established. He worked in Westchester as a facilities manager for Prodigy, but when he was home he was like the mayor of the Hudson Valley! Michael had two children with his wife, Betty. Michelle was about the same age as my daughter Jessica, and Brian was about the same age as my son Adam. Our children went to school in the same Wappinger's Central School District, but to the two different high schools in the district, John Jay and Ketcham.

Shortly after we made our connection Michael announced that he was getting a divorce. This news saddened me when I first heard it because we really liked his wife Betty. As it turns out Michael and his new wife Amelia, and Betty, get along very well. We invite Betty to all of our family functions and she and MaryAnn have a 'shop till you drop" tradition during each Christmas season. She's a sweetheart. Amelia also has a great heart. She made such a deep connection with Mary that you would think she was Mary's daughter. Amelia is a very caring and generous person.

Vinny worked at a Lumber Yard on Long Island

as a driver when we first met. He lived alone. Vinny was married for a short time, and then divorced. And then the unbelievable happened. Vinny won the New York State Lottery and a grand prize of nine million dollars! After taxes, Vinny walked away with $3.8 million! He married a lovely girl named Laura who comes from a very successful and loving family. They have one child, Vinny junior, and live on Long Island.

Vinny poses after winning the New York State Lottery

Hey Mom, Guess What?

I DID FINALLY TELL MY mother, Emily, that I met Mary and my brothers. She was both amazed and happy for me! I mentioned to her that I was a little reluctant to tell her because I didn't want her to think that I was searching because of some void she had left in my life. Her response was priceless. She looked at me and simply said, "No, that's silly. I know you love me." She had so many questions and seemed genuinely excited, happy, and amazed that this was actually happening.

Shortly after my initial meeting with the Cosentinos, Mike and I arranged a family reunion with all of the spouses and children, and BOTH Mary and Emily.

It was interesting to see my two moms together, and I thought things were going surprisingly well until a few days later when Emily confided in me that she felt uncomfortable in that setting and didn't want to do it again. I respected that and other than my daughter Jessica's wedding day, this was the only time Emily and Mary were seen together.

My adoptive mother Emily and my birth mother Mary

Mom died six months before I started writing this book. It was November of 2012; she was eighty-nine. When I think of all the sacrifices, and all the caring, the love, and the support she gave to me and the rest of my family, I cry. Ironically, while all this was happening, I was afraid it might make my mother feel that she wasn't enough of a mother to me, and now I find myself wondering if I was enough of a son to her. There is an adoption poem by Fleur Conkling Heyliger that fits my mother's love for me perfectly. A portion of the poem goes,

> *Not Flesh of My Flesh, Nor Bone of My Bone*
> *But Heart of My Heart, And Soul of My Soul*

Kendall, Melissa, Emily, Kalen, Kim, Mom, Adam, Erin, Jessica, and me on the Walkway Over the Hudson, 2009

More Discoveries

AFTER EMILY DIED, MY SISTER came across some old files in my mother's safe deposit box. Within those files were the original papers and correspondence leading up to my adoption, including typed letters to Catholic Charities written by my parents, correspondence from lawyers and the Surrogate's Court of Bronx County. But what struck me most was a handwritten letter by my father, Matthew.

722 East 228th Street
Bronx 66, New York
January 5, 1956

The Catholic Home Bureau
For Dependent Children
122 East 22nd Street
New York 10, New York

Att: Rev. G. Howard Moore:

Dear Father Moore:

We have received your most welcome letter informing us that we were again approved for legal adoption of Paul Henry Consortio who we call Charles Cornelius. With the Grace of God we will bring him up to be a good Catholic who will be a credit to all concerned.

We want to again express our sincere thanks to you and all your associates who have always treated us with the highest respect and courtesy. May God bless the wonderful work that is being done by your Bureau.

We would like to retain Mr. ____ as our adoption counsel, whom we are well acquainted with.

This draft is part of the letters that were written between January 25, 1955 and April 6, 1956. It appears that, while I always thought I was adopted on December 23, 1954, I was actually fostered until the adoption became official on March 13,

1956. This was the letter written to Catholic Charities Home Bureau almost a year after I had been living with my adopted parents. The purpose of this correspondence was to officially request legal adoption.

Mrs. Matthew Cornacchio
722 East 228th Street
Bronx 66, New York

November 27, 1955

The Catholic Home Bureau
122 East 22nd Street
New York 10, NY

Gentlemen:

I have always wanted a family since we had our little girl, whom we legally adopted in March 1954, we decided we would like to adopt a little boy.

We have this child whom we call

Charles, in our home for nearly a year, and we all dearly love him and desire that he remain here permanently.

We will always try to guide him in the right path and see that he has everything that he needs. He will start his education at the Our Lady of Grace School, which has been my parish since I was his age.

We have started a bank account for him, which we pray with the Lord's Blessing will grow with the years, so that if he desires to go on with his studies it will be within his reach.

I sincerely hope that you will find everything in order and grant that Charles can remain with us.

Sincerely,
Mrs. Matthew Cornacchio

I could feel my parents' sense of urgency and their anxiety. I thought about how they must have felt as the adoption agency performed its home investigations, and how difficult it must have been to write these letters only to sit around and wait for a response. In our current age of immediacy, we will never know what it's like to drop a letter of hope into a mailbox and wait in silence for a reply that might take weeks, or even months.

The paper is faded but, oddly, still has a scent of the perfume my mother wore. I can't tell you what it was, but as I lifted the paper to my nose, the smell took me back to our row house on 235th street when I was a boy.

～

Mary passed away while I was finishing this book. She started to develop health issues consistent with old age, some scattered thoughts, and a couple of mild strokes. At 86, Mary was in and out of the hospital. On the day she died, Mary was in the hospital but feeling much better and had a burst of energy. When her second husband, Bob, arrived, he was happily surprised to see Mary in such a good mood and vibrant. Bob offered to go home and get a fresh set of clothes so Mary could walk around the halls rather than being confined to her room in a hospital gown. But when Bob came back, Mary was gone.

She apparently suffered from an overabundance of lung fluid coupled with another stroke. Mary was 86.

With Mary at Vinny's wedding

Mary (Consentino) Ball died on September 14, 2013. She is survived by a husband, Robert Ball, who coincidentally worked with my biological father at Neptune Movers. Her obituary reads:

Mary P. Ball, a longtime resident of New Rochelle, died on September 14, 2013. She was 86.

Mary was born on April 24, 1927, in Mamaroneck to the late Joseph and Angelina (Rigano) Lanza. She worked for over 25 years as a waitress at the Larchmont Diner. She is survived by her husband Robert Ball; her sons Michael Cosentino, Robert Cosentino, Vincent Cosentino, and Charles Cornacchio; her 14 grandchildren; her 12 great-grandchildren; her sister Theresa Alberico and her brother Joseph Lanza. She was predeceased by her son Louis Cosentino and her brothers Charles, Anthony, Vincent, and Frank Lanza.

I am so grateful to have met Mary. I wish I would have known her in her younger years. By the time we finally reunited, she was plagued with knee pain. But in pictures of her in her twenties and thirties, I could tell she was a firecracker. I hold no grudges or animosity towards Mary. I do not judge her by any of her actions. We have all done things in our youth that we might have approached differently with the advantage of maturity.

What I admired about Mary was that she said what was on her mind, and, for better or worse, you always knew where you stood with her. She was a hard worker. It was completely clear that she loved her family and her extended family. She always made us feel welcomed. Mary was generous and caring, and she had a great sense of humor.

Divine Intervention

I BELIEVE OUR LIVES ARE predetermined. The choices
we make can alter the immediate outcome, but
God is ultimately in control. To this end, I believe
that there are many clear-cut examples of predeter-
mining how I met my mother, and that the timing
of this event was destiny.

I don't believe that the speed at which the facts
began to flow regarding my adoption were completely a coincidence. Getting the sportscaster job
was definitely instrumental in giving me the visibil-
ity for Mike to take notice.

Sports 1 celebrates 1-year anniversary

Executive producer Charlie Cornacchio, on the set of his regional sports show, has fulfilled a personal dream with the creation of Sports 1.

Local program off to successful start

By Ken McMillan
Poughkeepsie Journal

something anybody would love to be in that position. It's

one half-hour every weekday.

"It's a miniature takeoff of ESPN SportsCenter" said local sportscaster Dean Dar-

seen on three cable systems in the Mid-Hudson Valley covering much of Dutchess, Ulster, Putnam and Orange

face of the show. He was the show's creator, the executive producer and the anchor

"I was getting arrested 45 when we hit a small

Surely my story can appear as a "right place, right time" scenario based on how things happened. But to me, the timing of these events is spiritual. Consider all of them:

Sister Saint Paul ran the adoption ward at Misrecordia Hospital for over thirty years. In that time, there were no connections regarding my birth family, but within a year of her passing, connections began to appear. Could it be that she finally had the spiritual power to help bring us together?

My birth father died just three months before I met Mary. I wonder how different it might have been if I was able to approach Bob Harris after meeting Mary. Would he have put a negative slant on how well each encounter was going? Would bad feelings resurface?

Any number of slight deviations in how my life played out could have changed everything else and prevented me from finding the answers to my questions.

When you think of the many circumstantial events that had to happen to get me to the door of Mary's apartment and how one misstep could have prevented this completely unique discovery, you can get an appreciation of how fragile our life encounters and events can be. Knowing what my life is and what could have been if different paths were chosen makes this kind of my own *It's A Wonderful Life* story.

My path to discovery was spiritually orchestrated, and each event was built on a previous, seemingly unrelated event.

- **Beginning at birth:** If Mary had gotten her way and convinced her husband Louis to allow her to take me home at birth, my life would not have been blessed with the support and nurturing environment that my adoptive family showed me.

- **My adoption:** If my mother had listened to the doctor in those first three days of bringing me home and had given me back to the adoption agency, who knows where I would have ended up.

- **My father's death:** This forced my mother to move from our Bronx home to Valhalla to be closer to her sister and family. This is where I would meet my wife, MaryAnn, and together we would have four beautiful children and eight grandchildren. I can see how each of my children and grandchildren have affected other people's lives.

- **The job at MCI:** This is the job that helped me afford to buy a house that was coincidentally in the same town as my brother Michael.

It also exposed me to the opportunity of video editing, which helped me get the job at the cable TV company that ultimately led to the start of this amazing discovery

- **Cable TV job:** This job put my face on the TV and caused Michael to notice the uncanny resemblance. My coverage of the triathlon led to the awards banquet and forced our first face-to-face meeting.

How close we came ...

There were many times where my path could have crossed with other members of my birth family without us even knowing it. For example ...

- I worked directly across the street from my birth father in New Rochelle. While I was at American White Cross Labs on Webster Avenue, Robert Harris worked at Neptune Movers also on Webster Avenue.

Neptune movers on left, American White Cross Labs on right, Webster Avenue, New Rochelle

- Each time I took the field, while playing on the America White Cross company softball team, I stood directly beneath my birth mother's apartment window.

- I often walked by the Cosentino's dry cleaning business on Main Street in New Rochelle during my lunch breaks.

- My brother Michael and I both moved sixty miles north to the same small town. For ten years, we were just one mile down the road from each other before the connection was made.

My family, 2012

Some Thoughts for You

I WROTE THIS BOOK IN the hopes that it would give adopted people a sense of settlement. My experience when sharing my story was that everyone was amazed by the circumstances that led to the discovery, but it wasn't until Eliza, an adopted Russian girl heard it, that I realized that my story can help people feel a sense of resolve about their own adoption and typical questions that we all have.

Eliza was just a baby when Chris and Dave Rudolph brought her home. It was a difficult and expensive Russian adoption for the Rudolph's. But they were determined to do this and committed to being parents and helping out a child less fortunate.

Their timing was perfect for their adoption of

Eliza because in December of 2012 Russia passed a law that prevents U.S. Citizens from adopting Russian children.

Chrissy and my wife MaryAnn are lifelong friends since the second grade. At a recent visit, Chrissy asked me to share this story with her husband, Dave, because he hadn't heard the full version of it.

I told Dave an abridged version of the story you just read. At the end of it, Dave was tearing up. I realized it moved him like many others who have heard this story. I didn't realize that Eliza was listening as intently as she sat next to her father because she never made eye contact with me. I didn't think she was that interested.

After I was done telling the story, Chrissy asked if I had written it down. I told her that, in the early stages of the story developing, I started to write a screenplay because everyone who heard it said it sounded like a movie. But my attempt at creatively embellishing an already intriguing story got in the way and so I stopped.

About two weeks later Chrissy came up to me

at my daughter Kim's bridal shower and seemed so excited.

"I cannot tell you how much your story helped Eliza!" she blurted. "You should have heard her on the way home from your house after you told Dave the story! She kept talking about it!"

I was surprised because I really didn't even think she was listening.

"No, she heard every word," Chrissy continued. "You know, as a teenager now, she's been going through some issue about the whole adoption thing and wondering what her life would have been like if she had stayed in Russia, or if her parents had kept her." It was clear that the story had a profound effect on this girl.

And then Chrissy expressed relief when she said, "But the best part was about a week ago she said to me, "You know Mom, I'm okay with where I'm at. I don't care about what could have been. I know I'm in the best place I can be." Chrissy was tearing up as she relayed the conversation and that poignant moment.

You see, while adoptees are always wrestling

with feeling accepted by their surrounding world, we don't realize that adopting parents are wrestling with the same feelings of acceptance of their adopted children. It was crystal clear that moment was a monumental breakthrough for Chrissy and Dave, as adopting parents. And the feeling that Chrissy was expressing to me became my inspiration to actually take her advice and "put it down on paper." How rewarding it would be if I could help an adoptee or adopting parent feel the emotion and joy that Chrissy and Eliza felt because of this story.

Adoption comes with many questions and many emotions that only those of us who have been adopted can understand. There is a quiet emptiness and hole in our lives with many unanswered questions that leave us wondering about our history and heritage.

For those of us who are fortunate enough to find some of these answers, the information hits like thunder and lightning. Answers to age-old questions are revealed, closing some loops and opening doors to relationships and revelations. But sometimes the answers are not as we've imagined or hoped. We all fantasize that our birth parents are living in a beautiful house with a white picket fence. That they have great jobs and are valued members of their community. We wonder what our lives would have been like if only they had kept us. But in most cases this fantasy is just that—fantasy. The reality is that we probably have it much better than we ever would have, had we not been given up for adoption. I am fortunate that in finding my birth mother I now know, definitively, what my life "would have" been like, compared to what it has been. Having this knowledge is very settling for me, and hopefully reading my story will help to settle your mind about this question as well.

In Good Company

HERE ARE JUST A FEW people you may recognize who were adopted. It is clear that their lives turned out pretty good!

STEVE JOBS, Founder of Apple was born in 1955 and adopted soon after. As an adult, Jobs traced his family history and learned that his biological parents who weren't married when Steve was born, did later marry. They had a daughter who Jobs developed a close relationship with before his passing in 2012.

DEBRA HARRY, musician and the lead singer of the '80s group Blondie was given up for adoption when she was three months old.

FAITH HILL, the popular singer/songwriter was adopted when she was only a few days old.

SCOTT HAMILTON, the olympic skater was adopted at six weeks old.

RAY LIOTA, the star actor in the movie *Good-fellas* and *Field of Dreams* was adopted at six months old. Later in life he hired a private detective to find his biological mother. They met in 1997 and Ray made two major discoveries, first, that he wasn't Italian, and second, that he had a half-brother.

SARAH MCLACHLAN, a singer/songwriter, who has sold over forty million albums worldwide, didn't find out she was adopted until she was nine years old. She later met her birth mother who had given Sarah up for adoption as a struggling 19-year-old artist.

TOMMY DAVIDSON, a successful African American comedian was adopted when he was two years old. He was adopted by a white civil rights worker, Barbara Davidson, and grew up with two white siblings and his adoptive mother.

DAVE THOMAS, the founder and CEO of Wendy's was adopted at six weeks old and lost his adoptive mother when he was five years old. As an advocate for adoption, Thomas founded the Dave Thomas Foundation for Adoption.

BABE RUTH, the famous Sultan of Swat spent his entire childhood in an orphanage.

Adoption Gets Some Mainstream Attention

In 1976, the governor of Massachusetts, Michael Dukakis, announced an Adoption Week for his state. Later that same year President Gerald Ford proclaimed that Adoption Week would be celebrated nationally.

According to Child Welfare Information Gateway, President Reagan proclaimed the first National Adoption Week in 1984.

As more and more states started to participate in Adoption Week it became clear that more time was needed for holding events and in 1995, President Clinton, proclaimed November as National Adoption Month.

National Adoption Month is a time to celebrate family and to bring about awareness that there are hundreds of thousands of children in foster homes awaiting adoption.

States, communities, and agencies hold events during the month to bring the need for families into public view.

A Matter of Resolve and Closure

I ENCOURAGE EVERY ADOPTED PERSON to seek out their parents and their history. But I caution you to think back to that Ann Landers advice column with the letter from a woman who successfully tracked down her birth parents and didn't like what she found. How heart-wrenching that her discovery led to such disappointment after years of searching with the hope and fantasy that she was going to find that white picket fence.

In her case, she might have been better off not knowing. But how are we to know if the truth will provide an outcome we desire or the outcome we fear?

It has been said that the naked truth is better than the best dressed lie.

Ask yourself if you are ready for whatever you might uncover. Be sure to be truthful with yourself before you start because the pain could scar you for life. The birth parents we imagine are just that, imagined. And the circumstances by which you were put up for adoption might be heartbreaking.

In many cases, it takes a tremendous act of courage and selflessness for a parent to give a child up for adoption. They are doing it so that the child could have a better life.

If you know your birth family, think of your life as it stands now, and what it might have been had you not been adopted? In most cases, I believe adoptees are much better off because their adoptive parents consciously opened their homes for them. People looking to adopt are looking for all the right reasons. They make excellent parents because they are ready for it.

Your adoptive parents chose to have a child.

That makes a big difference. They have prepared for you financially, and emotionally. They researched. They waited. They went to great lengths to bring you into a loving home.

That is a lot different than being born into a family that might not have planned for you. A family that will welcome you just the same, but might not have been ready for you, financially or emotionally. This is not to say that unplanned pregnancies are always a problem for birth parents or are any better or worse than planned pregnancies, but just to accentuate the fact that parents who adopt are at least as focused, committed, if not more so, than the most prepared birth parents.

My mother's choice to keep me, even with all the illness I showed in those first few days, illustrates the unconditional love adoptive parents have.

That is a very special degree of love.

I am one of the lucky ones.

The discovery of my new family and the knowledge of my past has enhanced my life greatly. I have four brothers and another mother. And while nothing can replace the emotional connection I have with my adoptive family and parents, equally nothing can replace the thrill of finding four brothers that I like and admire.

The extension of my family has brought new joy and friendships into my life. As brothers, we share events and happenings in our lives, have dinner together when our schedules match, and follow each other online using Facebook.

I feel more complete with a sense of belonging since I met my birth family. I feel less alone and hope my story gives you some insight on this journey, which, for me, had a beginning, middle, and, most importantly, an end.

The circumstances leading up to my discovery were pretty miraculous, and not at all conventional.

I didn't put any effort into this search prior to meeting Michael, and I made no financial investment to investigate and track the history of my birth. A couple of simple phone calls and a career in television helped uncover all of the mysteries. It was God, Sister St. Paul, and the face of Robert Harris who served it up on a plate for me.

I am thankful and humbled to be able to now tell the complete story of how I met my mother ... and the four brothers I never knew I had.

About the author

CHARLES CORNACCHIO IS A TELEVISION producer. Nominated for two New York Emmy Awards and winner of seven Telly Awards, he has also written, hosted, and produced several TV programs in the New York television market. He has been a sports anchor and broadcaster for twenty-three years.

An accomplished musician, Charles received an Axiem Award for an original composition honoring the first responders after 9-11. He has served on the boards of various nonprofit organizations and volunteered his time for the Anderson Center for Autism, the Southern Dutchess Chamber of Commerce, Make-A-Wish, the Goldberg Center, the American Red Cross, and many others. He is the father of four children, has eight grandchildren, and lives with his wife of forty years, MaryAnn, in Highland, New York.

Reference

Timeline of Adoption History

1851

Massachusetts passed the first modern adoption law, recognizing adoption as a social and legal operation based on child welfare rather than adult interests.

1868

Massachusetts Board of State Charities began paying for children to board in private family homes; in 1869 an agent was appointed to visit children in their homes. This was the beginning of "placing-out," a movement to care for children in families rather than institutions.

1872

The New York State Charities Aid Association was organized.

1898

The Catholic Home Bureau was organized in New York by the St. Vincent De Paul Society. It was the first Catholic agency to place children in homes rather than orphanages, a model soon followed in other cities.

1910-1930

The first specialized adoption agencies were founded.

1917

Minnesota passed the first law mandating social investigation of all adoptions (including home studies) and providing for confidentiality of adoption records.

1919

The Russell Sage Foundation published the first professional child placing manual.

1919 – 1929

The first empirical field studies of adoption gathered basic information about how many adoptions were taking place, of whom, and by whom.

1921

Child Welfare League of America formally renamed and organized. The league adopted a constitution that defined standard-setting as one of the organization's core purposes; American Association of Social Workers founded.

1935

Social Security Act included provision for aid to dependent children, crippled children's programs, and child welfare, which eventually led to a dramatic expansion of foster care.

1937 – 1938

First Child Welfare League of America initiative that distinguished minimum standards for permanent (adoptive) and temporary (foster) placements.

1948

The first recorded transracial adoption of an African American child by white parents took place in Minnesota.

1949

New York was the first state to pass a law against black market adoptions, which proved unenforceable in practice.

1953 – 1954

Child Welfare League of America conducted nationwide survey of adoption agency practices

1953 – 1958

The first nationally coordinated effort to locate adoptive homes for African American children. The National Urban League Foster Care and Adoptions Project was formed.

1961

The Immigration and Nationality Act incorporated. For the first time, provisions are made for the international adoption of foreign-born children by U.S. citizens.

1965

The Los Angeles County Bureau of Adoptions launched the first organized program of single parent adoptions.

1969

President Nixon created the Office of Child Development.

1970

Adoptions reach their century-long statistical peek at approximately 175,000 per year. Almost 80 percent of the total were arranged by agencies.

1971

Florence Fisher founded the Adoptees Liberty Movement Association "to abolish the existing practice of sealed records and advocate for opening of records to any adopted person over eighteen who wants, for any reason, to see them.

1972

National Association of Black Social Workers opposed transracial adoptions; Stanley vs. Illinois substantially increased the rights of unwed fathers in adoption by requiring informed consent and proof of parental unfitness prior to termination of parental rights.

1973

Roe v. Wade legalized abortion.

1976

Concerned United Birthparents founded.

1978

Indian Child Welfare Act passed by congress.

1994

Multiethnic Placement Act was the first federal law to concern itself with race in adoption. It prohibited agencies receiving federal funds from denying transracial adoptions on the sole basis of race.

1996

Bastard Nation founded. It's mission statement promoted "the full human and civil rights of adult adoptees" including access to sealed records.

1997

Adoption and Safe Families Act stressed permanency planning for children and represented a policy shift away from family reunification and toward adoption.

1998

Oregon voters passed Ballot Measures 58, allowing adult adoptees access to original birth certificates. This legal blow to confidentiality and sealed records was stalled by legal challenges to the measure's constitutionality, which eventually failed. The measure has been in effect in Oregon since June 2000.

2000

The Child Citizenship Act of 2000 allowed foreign-born adoptees to become automatic American citizens when they entered the United States, eliminating the legal burden of naturalization for international adoptions.

2013

Russian President Vladimir Putin signed into law a measure that bans the adoption of Russian children by U.S. families, effective January 1, 2014. According to the U.S. State Department, Americans adopted close to one thousand Russian children in 2012.

CPSIA information can be obtained at www.ICGtesting.com
Printed in the USA
BVOW04s0037270315

393535BV00001B/1/P

9 781627 870580